Published by Kajuda Promotions Ltd., Barrie, Ontario Canada
December 2006
Printed and Bound in Canada
lee@dignam.com
705-721-1851

ISBN 0-9738603 1-6

Lee's Official "Chuckles" Book

BY LEE VASS

My greatest blessings call me "Gannie"

Dedicated to:
David Robin,
Graeme,
Kaileigh, Rosalee
and Sophie.

Founded in 1916, the H.M. Dignam Corporation Ltd. of Barrie, Ontario has been buying and selling country properties across Canada for many decades. Their customers are people interested in recreational acreages - not only for summer cottages but also for hunting, fishing, minerals, timber, investments, etc.

In 1987, they began a monthly newsletter to be sent out with their "Property Lists" and asked me to be the editor - which I gladly accepted. At the same time, someone made the suggestion that a humour column would add to the content because most people liked to laugh. I couldn't have agreed with them more because I love to laugh and do a great deal of it. Naturally, as editor, I was given the "fun" job of coming up with amusing stories, anecdotes, poems...whatever I could find to make people smile.

From the beginning I had strict guidelines to follow - no naughty stories, just good, clean, old fashioned reasons to giggle and most importantly, a guideline I made myself follow, (and the hardest test of all) - I had to think that each particular inclusion was truly funny or amusing. Once or twice I was tempted to include a naughty tale or two that was excruciatingly funny, but was always reminded that "we are an old-fashioned, conservative, family-oriented company and the newsletter must reflect this in its content."

It became great fun as I researched every possible source for the funniest jokes or whatever I could find to make you smile. I stuck to my policy of only including the stories I found amusing....maybe you missed some good ones because of that policy but "to thine own self be true" and I was.

Now celebrating their 90th anniversary, the folks at Dignam asked if I would put together a printed version of those many Chuckles down through the years. Once again I was delighted to oblige!

Here it is folks - all those jokes I found funny enough to print. Here's hoping they bring a chuckle or two to those of you who receive this printed "history" of the Chuckles column from the Dignam Country Window newsletters and their monthly property lists.

Enjoy !

Lee Vass

Chuckles

A surgeon, an engineer and a politician were debating which of their professions was the oldest. "Eve was made from Adam's rib" said the surgeon, "and before that, order was created out of chaos" said the engineer, "and that most certainly was an engineering job." "Ah-ha!" exclaimed the politician triumphantly, "and just who do you think created the chaos?"

THOUGHT FOR THE DAY

The road to success always seems to be under construction.

September is when millions of shining, happy faces turn toward school. They belong to mothers.

Anybody who thinks there's plenty of room at the top has a lot to learn about pyramids!

Anyone who calls a rose by any other name is probably pruning.

Daffy-nitions

AFTERNOON NAP: Matinee idle
SAILING: The art of getting wet and becoming ill while slowly going nowhere at great expense.
TORNADO: A hurricane that can't afford Florida

Sign Posted in Parry Sound Campground

If you with litter will disgrace and spoil the beauty of this place,
May indigestion rack your chest and ants invade your pants and vest!

☻ Hear about the restaurant they just opened on the moon? Great food, no atmosphere.

☻ Almost 500 years ago Columbus set out for the East Indies and wound up in the Caribbean. Today when you set out for the East Indies you get to the East Indies. It's your luggage that winds up in the Caribbean.

☻ In the 1930's people paid 10 cents to see a movie. Now they pay several hundred dollars for a TV set - and see the same movie.

☻ The junior college routinely cancels a course if fewer than 15 students register for it and "The American Revolution and the War of 1812" was thus threatened - until its savvy instructor changed the catalogue listing to read "13 Star Wars and the British Empire Strikes Back."

☻ A businessman dies. He goes immediately to the angel who guards the pearly gates and presents his business card. "Ah, yes, Mr. Johnson", the angel says. "Perhaps you could wait a minute while I consult our computer."
The angel returns in a moment with a sheaf of notes. "I'm afraid we don't seem to have a record of you performing any good deeds, Mr. Johnson. But I'm sure that a man of your reputation and integrity must have done something."
Mr. Johnson wishes his executive secretary was there. He racks his brain to think of some good deed that he can recount.
"Yes, let me see...I believe I gave a beggar a dime once. And I threw fifteen cents in the Salvation Army kettle last Christmas."
The angel excuses himself again and places a brief telex to the throne.
The answer comes back at once.
"I'm afraid we can't help you, Mr. Johnson," says the angel, "now or ever. The boss says "Give the guy back his quarter - and tell him to call the devil."

Poor Planning

This bricklayer's accident report was printed in the newsletter of the English equivalent of the Workers Compensation Board.

Dear Sir -

I am writing in response to your request for additional information on the accident reporting form.

I put "poor planning" as the cause of my accident. You said in your letter that I should explain more fully and I trust that the following details will be sufficient.

I am a bricklayer by trade. On the day of the accident, I was working alone on the roof of a new six-story building. When I completed my work, I discovered that I had about 500 pounds of bricks left over. Rather than carry the bricks down by hand, I decided to lower them in a barrel by using a pulley, which, fortunately, was attached to the side of the building at the sixth floor.

Securing the rope at ground level, I went up to the roof, swung the barrel out and loaded the bricks into it. Then I went back to the ground and untied the rope, holding it tightly to ensure a slow descent of the 500 pounds of bricks. You will note on the accident reporting form that my weight is 135 pounds.

Due to my surprise at being jerked off the ground so suddenly, I lost my presence of mind and forgot to let go of the rope. Needless to say, I proceeded at a rather rapid rate up the side of the building.

In the vicinity of the third floor, I met the barrel which was now proceeding in a downward direction at an equally impressive rate of speed. This explains the fractured skull, minor abrasions and the broken collarbone, as listed in Section III of the accident report. I continued my rapid ascent, not stopping until the fingers of my right hand were two knuckles deep into the pulley.

Fortunately by this time, I had regained my presence of mind and was able to hold tightly to the rope, in spite of the excruciating pain I was now beginning to experience. At approximately the same time, however, the barrel of bricks hit the ground - and the bottom fell out of the barrel.

Now devoid of the weight of the bricks, the barrel weighed approximately 50 pounds. As you might imagine, I began a rapid descent down the side of the building.

In the vicinity of the third floor, I met the barrel coming up. This accounts for the two fractured ankles, broken tooth and severe lacerations of my legs and lower body.

Here my luck began to change slightly.

The encounter with the barrel seemed to slow me enough to lessen my injuries when I fell into the pile of bricks - and, fortunately, only three vertebrae were cracked.

I am sorry to report, however, that, as I lay there on the pile of bricks in pain, unable to move and watching the empty barrel six stories above me, I again lost my composure and presence of mind and let go of the rope.

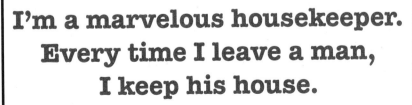

Sincerely,
Policy #XYR23456.

I'm a marvelous housekeeper.
Every time I leave a man,
I keep his house.
– Zsa Zsa Gabor

Chuckles

A woman was considering buying an aging thoroughbred but wanted a veterinarian's opinion of the horse before finalizing the deal. "Will I be able to race him?" she asked when the doctor had completed his examination. The vet looked at the woman, then at the horse. "Sure," he replied. "And you'll probably win."

Back in the old homesteading days, a parson once sold a horse to a member of his congregation. "She's a fine animal" he said, "but there are two things you have to remember. She's been well trained. When you want her to get going, say "Praise the Lord" and at "Amen" she will stop. The proud new owner saddled her up to ride her home and when they got out of town she broke into a gallop. Nothing he tried could slow her down - she kept right on going until they were racing toward the edge of a cliff... At last, he remembered what he's been told and screamed out "Amen, Amen" in the nick of time. The horse came to a stop not two feet from the ravine.

"Praise the Lord" said the thankful horseman.

Two boys walking in a field heard a buzzing sound near their feet. "Get away from there!" warned the local lad. "It's a rattlesnake! If you go near it, it'll strike!"

"No kidding," said his visitor from the city. "Do they have unions too?"

THESE STATEMENTS WERE ACTUALLY SUBMITTED TO INSURANCE COMPANIES ON CAR ACCIDENT REPORT FORMS:

"The telephone pole was approaching fast. I was attempting to swerve out of its path when it struck my front end."

"I was unable to control my car when it went berserk and struck another vehicle."

"The guy was all over the road. I had to swerve a number of times before I hit him."

"The pedestrian had no idea which direction to go, so I ran over him."

"A retarded cow struck my car and attempted to straddle my grill."

"I thought my window was down, but found it was up when I put my hand through it."

"I pulled away from the side of the road, glanced at my Mother-in-law and headed over the embankment."

"In my attempt to kill a fly, I drove into a telephone pole."

"My car was legally parked as it backed into the other vehicle."

"An invisible car came out of nowhere, struck my vehicle and vanished."

Chuckles

A highly competitive foursome was going around the golf course on a sweltering summer day. One of the group had a sun stroke - and the others made him count it.

After delivering two hours worth of meaningless campaign rhetoric, the candidate asked if anyone in the audience had a question. "Yeah", came a voice from the crowd. "Who else is running?"

The difference between education and experience is really quite similar: Education is what you get from reading the fine print. Experience is what you get from not reading it.

Young Ben protested heatedly when his mother insisted he take his little sister fishing with him. "Last time she came I couldn't catch a single fish!" "I'll talk to her " promised Mom. "She won't make any noise this time." "It wasn't the noise last time" Ben explained. "She ate all my bait."

AD FOR A HEALTH CLUB:
"Come in and dispose of your solid waist."

Young Jason attended his first ballet and as he watched the dancers move about on their toes, a puzzled look crossed his face. "Mommy," he finally whispered, "why don't they just get taller ladies?

The following are actual announcements which were printed in church bulletins - much to the amusement of the congregations in question, who were fortunately blessed with the ability to laugh at themselves and share the chuckle with us.

"This afternoon there will be services in the south and north ends of the church. Children will be baptized at both ends."

"This being Easter Sunday, we will ask Mrs. Johnson to come forward and lay an egg on the altar."

"Thursday at 5:00 p.m. there will be a meeting of the Young Anglican Mothers Club. All those wishing to become Young Anglican Mothers please meet the minister in his study after today's service."

"Next Sunday, a special collection will be taken to defray the expenses of the new carpet. All those wishing to do something on the new carpet, please come forward and get the necessary paper."

"The ladies of the church have cast off clothing of every kind and they may be seen in the church basement on Friday afternoon."

"A bean supper will be held Saturday evening in the church basement. Music will follow."

"The rosebud on the altar this morning is to announce the birth of David Allen Elser, the sin of The Rev. & Mrs. John B. Elser."

Chuckles

A doctor conducting a physical examination noticed bad bruises on the patient's shins. "Those from playing hockey or soccer?" asked the doctor. "Neither" replied the patient. "Bridge."

A fellow wrote to a mail order house. "Please send me the engine you show on page 878 and if it's any good, I'll send you a cheque." A week later he received the reply: "Please send cheque. If it's any good we'll send you the engine."

Daffy-nitions

BURGLAR ALARM: Protection racket.

MOSQUITO: Original skin diver.

PROPERTY DISPUTE: Ground beef.

SECONDHAND BOOKS: Twice sold tales.

INVENTION: Birth of a notion.

A patient confessed to her physician that she had first consulted a fortune teller, a faith healer and a palm reader. "And what foolish advice did they give you?" asked the doctor. The patient replied: "They all told me to see you."

One frog sitting on a lily pad said to another: "Time sure is fun when you're having flies."

● A customer whose chequebook was in total chaos phoned his bank for help. "What balance do you show?" asked the service representative. Came the harried reply, "I asked you first."

● Sign in clothing store: "Make sure the end justifies the jeans."

● An arrogant young woman wired home from her new job: "Made supervisor: feather in my cap."

A few weeks later she wired again: "Made manager: feather in my cap." Then after a few weeks more she sent another: "Fired: send money for ticket to fly home." Her parents wired back: "No ticket necessary. Use feathers."

● Sign on sandblaster truck: "Call us with your dirty storeys."

● Did you hear about the man who loses his temper over everything, no matter how trivial? He's a real Jack-of-all-tirades.

● The Sunday school lesson was about Noah's Ark and the teacher asked the children how they thought Noah might have whiled away those 40 long dreary days.

"I'll bet he spent a lot of time fishing" one youngster suggested. "He couldn't have," retorted his friend. "He only had two worms."

 *Chuckles*

MY DEAR GRANDSON:

Thank you for your letter. I'm pleased that you liked your birthday present and I appreciated your concern about my well-being. My health might be failing but let me remind you that we old folks are still worth a fortune. Why we have silver in our hair, gold in our teeth, stones in our kidneys, lead in our feet and gas in our stomachs. You ask what I am doing for excitement these days. Well a few changes have come into my life and I have become quite a frivolous old gal. As a matter of fact I am seeing five gentlemen every day. As soon as I wake up, Will Power helps me out of bed. Then I go to see John. At this point Charlie Horse comes along and when he leaves, Arthur Ritis shows up and stays the rest of the day. He doesn't like to stay in one place very long so he takes me from joint to joint. After such a busy day I'm really tired and glad to go to bed - usually with Ben Gay.

What a life!
Your loving Grandma.

P.S. The preacher came by the other day and said at my age I should be thinking about the here-after. I told him, "Oh I do that all the time. No matter where I am - in the parlor, upstairs, in the kitchen or down in the basement. I ask myself....Now what am I here after?"

A woman standing in a supermarket checkout line was pushed aside by another shopper who demanded that the cashier "Ring up my ten cans of cat food, quick!" Turning to the startled woman, the rude customer then said, "I hope you don't mind waiting."

"Oh, no," the woman replied, smiling sweetly. "Not if you're that hungry".

Daffy-nitions

VANITY FARE: Low calorie plate

DUCK HUNTER: What ducks try to do.

STATISTICS: Numbers looking for an argument.

FANATIC: A person who's enthusiastic about something in which you have no interest.

VIRUS: A Latin word used by doctors to mean "Your guess is as good as mine.

WEATHER BUREAU: Another non-prophet enterprise.

HIGH HEELS: Arch enemies

TACT: Intelligence of the heart.

ADULT: A person who has stopped growing at both ends and is now growing in the middle.

EGOTIST: Someone me-deep in conversation.

COTTAGE TIME

The family has been building to a fever pitch of excitement for the past week in anticipation of the cottage you rented on

the lake for this year's vacation. You have finally reached the rented premises after miles of twisting, turning country roads.

The key to the front door works - hooray! To greet you there is a letter propped on the mantlepiece (along with the spider webs and dead flies). It reads as follows:

Welcome to Whispering Pines

We know you're going to enjoy our cottage as much as we do and here's a few things to make your stay a pleasant one.

To get running water in the house simply call Mr. Ormond at 645-0609. He's a great fellow who knows our cottage plumbing better than we do. If it's during the day he might be at work in the local textile mill but he can always be reached after 5 p.m. If you have to use the "facilities" before then, just carry buckets of water from the lake and pour them down the john to manually flush it.

Once the water has been turned on you might find the kids are frightened by the sound of the pump (which is right beside the toilet and occasionally emits a screeching sound that is actually nothing more than air in the line but sounds pretty scary if you're not used to it). For this reason we don't recommend you flush the toilet or run water during the night - it could waken the family. Our kids play a game called "getting out of the bathroom before the pump goes on" and it has become great family fun. We suggest you teach it to any timid youngsters in your family.

For hot water in the kitchen tap, simply start a wood fire in the stove and this heats the water in the tank beside it. You might want to wait and do all your dishes at night as we do since it does tend to heat up the kitchen on hot days and makes it completely off limits for cooking.

It's a good idea to keep everything in the kitchen in tightly shut containers, or in the fridge, since ants have a way of finding a single grain of sugar left out on the counter - and you know those little devils - they work in long single lines to the outdoors. Plastic bags don't help much since the field mice nibble through a plastic bag lickity split. (You just can't keep those little rascals out.)

Our telephone ring is three long and two short - you have to listen carefully from the first ring but you will quickly get used to it. Since it is a six family party line, the ringing is fairly constant, especially in the morning on weekends when guests are calling for directions, but you'll find after the first week you just don't hear it anymore unless you are listening for your own ring. We don't suggest you have too many personal conversations on the telephone since it is a party line. Mrs. Arnold down the road, who is recuperating from a severe illness, sometimes behaves erratically where the phone is concerned. We ask that you be under-standing and patient with her. She's really a dear soul when she's well.

The television set works as long as it's not overcast on the lake. The color knob can be adjusted with a pair of long-nosed pliers. Since we only receive the local channel (#10) at least you don't have to worry about switching channels.

If the power goes out during a storm, there's a good supply of candles in a tin on the shelf over the kitchen sink and we would ask that you replace whatever you use for the family renting after you. (Please keep them in the tin because the mice like to eat these too.)

When you are down by the water, keep an eye out for the thin board near the end of the dock. We didn't have a chance to replace it last fall since Mr. Ormond's brother broke his ankle taking the dock in and couldn't make the repairs. (He promised to come by early this season and take care of it.)

Warn the kids about the dock spiders when sunbathing. They are black and hairy and look sort of like a tarantula. If you're out in the middle of the lake and one crawls out from under the bow of the rowboat, it can give you quite a turn. In the off chance you get nipped by one - apply ice immediately and get to the local hospital for an antihistamine shot. Those little devils can be powerful during their mating season.

The garter snakes you might see on the front lawn are harmless and are a sure sign the ecology of the lake is sound.

Should the dog next door make a pest of himself by growling at you, your children, or guests, simply try to ignore it since that family are totally incapable of a reasonable conversation when it comes to their children or animals. Their son tends to get a bit aggressive with his power boat when there are swimmers off our dock but after a bit he tires of the game and goes elsewhere. While he's up to his tricks we simply stay out of the water.

Garbage pickup is every other Friday at 7 a.m. and for some reason they are always here a little on the early side. We suggest you don't put it out the night before since the raccoons seem capable of opening any garbage can known to man and make quite a mess.

Enjoy your vacation.   *The Marstead family*

Chuckles

A boy was watching his father write a sermon. "How do you know what to say?" he asked. "Why, God tells me" the clergyman replied. "Oh", said the lad. "Then why do you keep crossing things out?"

Luke and Rodney were in a convenience store when a hoodlum rushed in brandishing a gun. "This is a hold-up!" he shouted. While the other patrons were being searched for valuables, Luke nudged his friend. "Take this" he whispered. "Take what?" hissed Rodney. "The twenty dollars I owe you."

A pickup truck pulled up to the barn and the driver hailed the farmer. "How much is that old bull out by the road worth to you?" he asked.

"Depends" drawled the farmer after a moment's hesitation. "Are you the tax assessor, do you want to buy him, or did you run him down with your truck?"

They've stopped teaching Latin in schools: how come they haven't stopped putting Roman numerals on Super Bowls?

Counselor to job seeker: "We'll have to emphasize your good points." "I was fired ten times." "What does that prove?" "I'm no quitter."

"Is your advertising getting results?" one store owner asked another. "Sure is" groaned his colleague. "Last week we advertised for a night watchman. The next night we were robbed."

Sign in window of auto muffler shop: "No appointment necessary. We hear you coming."

☺ A tourist in China was admiring a local man's necklace. "What's it made of?" she asked. "Alligator's teeth." "Well" she said, startled, "I suppose they hold the same value for you as pearls do for us." "Not really," the man answered. "Anybody can open an oyster."

☺ Two business owners talked right after both had negotiated sizable loans. "If conditions don't improve soon," said one, "I'll have to rob a bank." "If conditions don't improve soon," said the other, "I just did."

☺ Grass grows fastest during warm, damp weather - and when your lawnmower is on the blink.

☺ A man asked his wife how she liked his new rainbow-patterned tie. "Well" she responded, "I would like it even better if there wasn't such a big pot at the end of it."

☺ This sign in the Budapest Zoo lost something in the translation: "Please do not feed the animals. If you have any suitable food, give it to the guard."

☺ "We've had no trouble meeting our expenses," said the new homeowner. "Every time we turn around, there they are."

A noted playwright received a manuscript from an obvious novice. With the disjointed amateurish piece was a note that read: "Please read the enclosed and advise. Need answer at once as I have other irons in the fire." The playwright wrote back: "Remove irons. Insert manuscript."

An air traveller stopped at a machine to take out $100,000 worth of insurance before her trip. Next she stepped on a scale that gave her weight and fortune. She cringed when she read, "Your recent investment will pay off."

Sign above allergy remedy display:
"Buy now and avoid the rash."

● What do you call a boomerang that doesn't come back?
...A stick.

● A Dutchman was describing his country's red, white and blue flag to an American: "It's symbolic of our taxes," he said. "We turn red when we talk about them, white when we figure them and blue when we pay them." "Well whaddayaknow" exclaimed the American, "it's the same in the U.S. - only we see stars too."

● A son wanted to follow in his father's footsteps until he noticed that his Dad was wearing work boots instead of loafers.

● A woman, who had been married for fifty years to an eternal pessimist, died and went to heaven. It was more beautiful than she'd ever imagined! She couldn't wait to show it to her husband one year later when he arrived at the pearly gates. Taking him on a tour, she exclaimed "The sky, the flowers, the music, the people - have you ever seen anything so perfect? Heaven is truly heaven, isn't it?" He surveyed paradise briefly and then said "Sure, and if it weren't for you and your doggoned oat bran, we'd have been here five years sooner."

● Automotive engineers in Russia tested castor oil as a possible replacement for diesel fuel. They eventually ruled it out because the cars had to make too many pit stops.

The will of a wealthy, but eccentric, man was being read and the relatives all listened expectantly. Finally the lawyer said, "And to my nephew, Charles Jones, whom I promised to remember in my will: Hi there, Charlie."

The day before Thanksgiving a magazine food editor received a call from a young lady, who identified herself as a new bride, who asked how long to roast a 20 lb turkey. "Just a minute," said the food editor as she turned to consult the chart on her bulletin board. "Thanks a lot!" said the young bride...and hung up.

Learn from the mistakes of others. You'll never live long enough to make them all yourself!

Postage stamps are getting more expensive, but at least they have one attribute that most of us could aspire to. They stick to one thing until they get there!

THE SAD TALE OF THE SUMMERTIME ANGLER

To catch the fish I've got the gear. A rod, a reel and a case of beer.

A fishing boat to get me there.
Twelve dozen plugs and lures to spare.
There's just one thing that's bugging me.
I've added and subtracted 'til I can't see.
With all my equipment, I have found
A fish costs fifty bucks a pound!

MORE STATEMENTS ACTUALLY SUBMITTED TO INSURANCE COMPANIES ON ACCIDENT REPORT FORMS.

"The other driver struck my car with an expired Drivers License, then left the scene of the accident."

"I had been shopping for plants all day and was on my way home. As I reached an intersection, a hedge sprang up obscuring my vision and I did not see the other car."

"The other driver looked like the usual lane-hopping type with thick horn-rimmed glasses, pimply face, brown suit and thick soled shoes."

"Upon collision and in a flash of blue, I hit my head, twisted my neck and tossed the lower part of my body out the side window."

"I had been driving my car for forty years when I fell asleep at the wheel and had the accident."

"I was thrown from my car as it left the road. I was later found in a ditch by some strange cow."

"I thought I could squeeze between two trucks when my car became squashed."

"The accident happened when the right front door of a car came around the corner without giving a signal."

"When I pressed the windshield spray button, my car left the road and struck a fire hydrant. I was unable to see the road because of the spray."

"The accident occurred when I was attempting to bring my car out of a skid by steering it into the other vehicle."

"I struck the young man with my husband's car. He wanted to call the police but after having a look at my particulars he decided we would go to his apartment and settle things."

A flea once lived on a pheasant
Who was royally vain and unpleasant
'Til the flea, on a whim,
Bit the "h" out of him;
And now he is only a peasant.

☺ The loaded station wagon pulled into the only remaining campsite. Four youngsters leaped from the vehicle and began feverishly unloading gear and setting up a tent. The boys then rushed off to gather firewood, while the girls and their mother setup the camp stove and cooking utensils.

A nearby camper marveled to the youngsters' father: "That, sir, is some display of teamwork." "I have a system," the father replied, "no one goes to the bathroom until the camp is set up."

☺ A hungry lion prowling the jungle came upon two men sitting under a tree. One was reading a book while the other pecked away at a typewriter. The lion immediately pounced upon the man with the book and gobbled him up - for the king of beasts knew that readers digest, but writers cramp.

☺ To err is human. To really mess up, you need a computer.

The lion may well
lie down with the lamb,
but the lamb
won't get much sleep!"

CUSTOMER TO TV SALESMAN:
I don't need a remote-control television. With four kids, my chances of controlling it are already remote.

Once upon a time there were three bears, Momma Bear, Poppa Bear and little Baby Bear. On this particular evening the Bear family were sitting down to dinner when the front door crashed open and in strode a ferocious strange looking bear brandishing a revolver.

He ran over to the dinner table, quickly emptied all of the plates of food into his huge jaws, fired a shot in the air with the revolver he carried and just as rapidly as he had entered, he went out the door, slamming it firmly behind him.

The three mystified bears looked at each other in amazement. Poppa Bear said - "Well I'll be.......what on earth kind of a bear do you suppose that was?"

Without a moment's hesitation, bright little Baby Bear announced "Why that must have been a Koala Bear." Momma and Poppa Bear were dumbfounded and asked "Why Baby Bear, whatever makes you think so?"

"It's right here in my Book of Bear Facts" answered Baby Bear. "On Page 4 it says "Koala Bear, eats shoots and leaves.""

I eat my peas with honey, I've done so all my life
They may taste rather funny,
but it sticks them to my knife

SIGNS

A sign posted on a corner in Geneva: "The parade will take place in the morning if it rains in the afternoon."

Seen in an African hotel: "A room with a view of the sea or the backside of the country."

A clothing store sign in Brussels: "Come inside and have a fit."

On the menu of a Polish hotel: "Salad a firm's own make; limpid red beet soup with cheesy dumplings in the form of a finger; roasted duck let loose; beef rashers beaten up in the country people's fashion."

In a Budapest hotel lobby: The lift is being fixed for the next day. During that time we regret that you will be unbearable.

DON'T FORGET

✔ Diplomacy is the art of saying "Nice doggie" until you can find a rock.

✔ Time is nature's way of keeping everything from happening at once.

✔ Wrinkles merely indicate where smiles have been.

✔ If you think no one cares if you're alive or dead, try missing a few payments.

✔ Cats are smarter than dogs. You could never get eight cats to pull a sled through snow.

Chuckles

OVERHEARD DURING THE RECESSION: "You think your job is shaky. In my office they pass out the desk calendars in weekly installments."

On returning to her car in a parking lot, a lady found the door on the driver's side punched in and a note on the windshield which read as follows: "I'm writing this because a dozen people are watching me. They think I'm leaving you my name and address but I'm not."

● We may not return the affection of those who like us...but we respect their good judgment.

● Definition of overeating: Exceeding the feed limit.

● Know what happens when you cross a kangaroo with a sheep? You get a wool sweater with very large pockets.

● Ned and Joe had been close since childhood. They played on the same ball teams, married sisters and built homes in the same neighbourhood.
When Ned died, Joe was lost and grief stricken. One evening, watching a beautiful sunset, Joe was sure he felt the presence of Ned nearby. "Is that you, Ned?" he asked. "Yes, Joe" came the reply.
    "What's it like where you are?" "Well, it's kind of nice. I get up in the morning, have some breakfast, maybe go for a swim in the lake. When I encounter a lovely lady I enjoy a romantic interlude. Soon, it's time for lunch and a nap."
    "Wow" said Joe. "I had no idea heaven was like that."
    "Who says I'm in heaven" replied Ned. "I'm a moose in Alberta."

😊 Anthropologists have discovered a 50 million year old skull with three perfectly preserved teeth intact. They're not sure, but they think it may be the remains of the very first hockey player.

😊 Oldtimer's definition of today's rock bands: "Music depreciation."

😊 During a break in the recital, the tenor advised his audience "Five years ago I insured my voice with Lloyd's of London for one million dollars."
Overheard in the hush that followed this announcement was a lady enquiring "Wonder what he did with the money?"

😊 Hear about the psychiatrist who got a late night call from a kleptomaniac patient? The patient was advised, "take two ashtrays and call me in the morning."

😊 Meteorologists have figured out why Buffalo, N.Y. gets such a bad time of it in the winter. It is located at the exact point where the cold air coming down from Canada meets all the hot air coming up from Washington.

😊 An elephant was drinking from a river in the jungle when he spotted a snapping turtle asleep on a log. He walked over to the creature and kicked it clear across the river. "Why did you do that" asked the giraffe. "Because" explained the elephant," he was the turtle who nipped my trunk fifty years ago."
"Wow, what a memory" said the giraffe.
"Yes" replied the elephant, "Turtle recall."

Chuckles

A diamond is a piece of coal that made good under pressure.

"After two years of therapy, you are completely cured" the psychiatrist told his lady patient. Noting the frown on her face, he asked "What's wrong with that? I thought you would be very happy with my pronouncement."

"Oh great!" the woman replied sarcastically. "Two years ago I was Cleopatra and now I'm a nobody."

LIFE IS TOO SHORT TO STUFF MUSHROOMS.

A woman drove a mini-van filled with a dozen screaming kids through the mall parking lot, looking for a space. Obviously frazzled, she coasted through a stop sign. "Hey lady, have you forgotten how to stop?" yelled an irate man. She rolled down the window and said "What makes you think they're all mine?"

Do you know why they hang mistletoe over the baggage counter at airports during the holiday season?
So you can kiss your luggage goodbye.

Wild rabbit is delicious sautéed, stewed or baked, but don't use it in a gumbo........... No one likes hare in their soup!

A deer and a lion came into a restaurant and sat down at the counter. "I'll have a bowl of cereal and a ham sandwich" said the deer. "Nothing for me" said the lion. "What's the matter?" the waiter asked the lion, "Aren't you hungry?"
"If he were hungry" said the deer, "would I be sitting here?"

THE TROUBLE WITH UNEMPLOYMENT IS THAT THE MINUTE YOU WAKE UP YOU'RE ON THE JOB.

A fellow walked into a doctor's office and the receptionist asked him what he had. He said "Shingles". So she took down his name, address, medical insurance number and told him to take a seat. Fifteen minutes later a nurse's aide came out and asked him what he had. He said "Shingles". So she gave him a blood test, blood pressure check, an electrocardiogram and a urine test and told him to take off all his clothes and wait for the doctor.

An hour later the doctor came in and asked him what he had. He said "Shingles". "Where?" asked the doctor.

"Outside on the truck" answered the fellow. "Where do you want them?"

A couple whose passion had waned consulted a marriage counselor. Several appointments later, after little success, the therapist suddenly swept the woman into his arms and kissed her.

"You see," the counselor said to the husband, "this is the treatment your wife needs at least thee nights a week."

"Well" replied the husband, "I can bring her in here any night but Monday, that's my bowling night."

Chuckles

A man trying to understand the nature of God asked him some questions: "God, how long is a million years to you?" and God said, "A million years is like a minute." Then the man asked, "God, how much is a million dollars to you?" and God said, "A million dollars is like a penny." The man thought for a moment and asked "God, will you give me a penny?" and God said, "In a minute."

TALK IS CHEAP BECAUSE THE SUPPLY EXCEEDS THE DEMAND

A doctor died and went to heaven where he found himself at the end of a long line to enter the pearly gates. As he normally did on earth, he rushed up to the front of the line and, expecting the usual preferential entry status, announced to St. Peter. "I'm a doctor."

St. Peter told him that he had to wait in line like everyone else. A short time later an elderly man, wearing a white coat and stethoscope and carrying a black bag, walked up to the front of the line and St. Peter immediately admitted him through the pearly gates.

"What's going on here?" shouted the doctor from the end of the line. "How come you let him through so fast?" "Well, you see" said St. Peter, "that's God, and sometimes he likes to play doctor."

A small boy grabbed his coat and boots. "Mom", he asked, "can I go outside and help Dad put the snow chains on the car? I know all the words."

Overheard in the veterinarian's waiting room: "I had my cat neutered last month. He still stays out all night with the other cats, but now it's in the role of consultant."

🙂 After paying $700 for a new suit, a young lady was very upset when she saw the same suit in a nearby store for $150. She promptly went back to the place of purchase to complain.

"Really, Miss, the copy of our suit which you saw is not 100 percent virgin wool." "For that much difference in the price" said the irate customer, "I really don't care what the sheep do at night."

🙂 A policeman pulled over an elderly driver and said, "My gosh, man, didn't you realize your wife fell out of the car 3 miles back?"

"Thanks be to God", exclaimed the old gent, "I thought I'd gone deaf."

Three vampires strolled into a pub and sat down at the bar. "What'll it be?" asked the bartender.
"I'll have a glass of blood," said the first. "So will I" the second vampire concurred.
"And I'll have a glass of plasma," requested the last.
"Okay," the barkeep replied.
"That'll be two bloods and a blood lite."

 *Chuckles*

EXCERPTS FROM ACTUAL LETTERS RECEIVED AT ONE OF THE REGIONAL TAX OFFICES OF REVENUE CANADA

- "If my husband puts in a claim for a dependent named Marcia, I just want you to know that my name is Gertrude."

- "Please keep my refund until further notice. My wife wants to use it to bring her mother over from the Old Country."

- "I don't know why you should be interested in the length of my residence in Quebec, but I have nothing to hide. It is 31 feet, 8 inches long and there's an attached garage."

- "I cannot pay the full amount at the moment as my husband is in hospital. As soon as I can, I will send the remains."

-- "I'll tell you what I tell every taxpayer who sits in that chair," said the Revenue Canada agent at the beginning of Joe Smith's audit. "It's a privilege to live in this great country, and you should pay your taxes with a smile."

"Thank goodness" said a visibly relieved Smith. "I thought you were going to ask for money."

I drink too much!
Last time I gave a urine sample
there was an olive in it..
Rodney Dangerfield

> **IF NOAH HAD BEEN TRULY WISE**
> **HE WOULD HAVE SWATTED THOSE TWO FLIES.**

OVERHEARD:

"The government keeps saying the economy is on the right track. There's only one problem–the train isn't moving!"

"Isn't five hundred dollars a lot of money for a sweater?" asked a customer. "Not really," the store clerk replied. "The sweater's wool was shorn from sheep whose habitat is the most inaccessible area of the Himalayas. It is truly an amazing yarn." "And," commented the shopper, "You tell it so well!"

A gentleman entered a busy florist shop that displayed a large sign that read "Say it with flowers". "Wrap up one rose," he told the salesgirl. "Only one?" asked the florist. "Just one. I'm a man of few words."

GRAFFITI UNDER A **"DRINK CANADA DRY"** SIGN:
"Lord knows, I've tried!"

To impress his date, the young man took her to a very chic Italian restaurant. After sipping some fine wine, he picked up the menu and ordered. "We'll have the Guiseppe Spomdalucci," he said. "Sorry, sir," said the waiter, "That's the proprietor."

At a plush hotel, a fellow walked up to the front desk and asked the desk clerk, "Do I register with you?"
"Not by any stretch of the imagination," snapped the woman.

Chuckles

Question: What do you call a politician who has lost an election?
Answer: A consultant.

🙂 Have you heard about the fellow who applied for a job where security was extremely important? They said they were looking for a guy who could keep his mouth shut. He told them he could. They said "Okay, we'll see," and started him out at less than minimum wage.

🙂 An Easterner walked into a Western saloon and was amazed to see a dog sitting at a table playing poker with three men. "Can that dog really read cards?" he asked. "Yeah, but he ain't much of a player," said one of the men. "Whenever he gets a good hand, he wags his tail.

🙂 A retired New England gentleman was sitting on the porch outside his home when a farmer approached with a wagon. "Good afternoon," said he to the farmer. "Afternoon," said the farmer. "Where are you headed?" asked the gentleman. "Town" said the farmer. "What do you have in the wagon?" "Manure" the farmer replied. "Manure, eh? That's interesting. What are going to do with it?" "Spread it over my strawberries," the farmer said. "Well," said the gentleman "you should come here for lunch someday. We use whipped cream."

🙂 A minister was on the golf course when he heard a duffer, deep in a sand trap, let loose a stream of profanity. "I have often noticed," chided the minister, "that the best golfers are not addicted to the use of foul language." "Of course not," screamed the golfer, "What do they have to swear about?"

NOTICES FROM AROUND THE GLOBE, WHICH HAVE PROVIDED MANY A SMILE TO THE WEARY NORTH AMERICAN TRAVELLER:

In a Paris hotel elevator:
Please leave your values at the front desk.

In a Yugoslavian hotel:
The flattening of underwear with pleasure is the job of the chambermaid.

Swiss Restaurant Menu:
Our wines leave you nothing to hope for.

In a Bangkok dry cleaners:
Drop your trousers here for best results.

In an East African Newspaper:
A new swimming pool is rapidly taking shape since the contractors have thrown in the bulk of their workers.

Posted in Germany's Black Forest:
It is strictly forbidden on our black forest camping site that people of different sex, for instance, men and women, live together in one tent unless they are married with each other for that purpose.

By a Hong Kong dentist:
Teeth extracted by the latest methodists.

In a Zurich hotel: *Because of the impropriety of entertaining guests of the opposite sex in the bedroom it is suggested that the lobby be used for this purpose.*

In the window of a Swedish furrier:
Fur coats made for ladies from their own skin.

In a Hong Kong Supermarket:
For your convenience, we recommend courteous, efficient self-service.

AIN'T IT THE TRUTH?

If at first you don't succeed, this is about normal.

Being single means you don't have to leave a party just when you are starting to have a good time.

Honesty is the best policy because it has so little competition.

"Health: To eat what you don't want, drink what you don't like, and do what you'd rather not."   Mark Twain

"It's necessary to go out on a limb sometimes because that's where the fruit is!"   Will Rogers

The advice you give a child is considered dumb until he gets the same advice from a buddy.

You know you're an oldtimer if you think that sunshine and bacon and eggs are good for you.

Even harder than breaking a bad habit is to refrain from telling people how you did it.

Knowledge is in the cities...but wisdom is in the woods.

Before you decide to retire, take a week off and watch daytime television.

Whoever uses the term "dirt cheap" probably hasn't bought any real estate lately.

A clear conscience is often the sign of a bad memory.

After giving birth to identical twins, the mother gave them up for adoption. A couple from Spain adopted one and named him "Juan". The other was adopted by a family from Egypt and they called their twin "Amal".

Years passed and the boy from Spain discovered his real mother and sent her a picture of himself. The woman remarked to her friend that she wished she also had a photo of her other son.

"Why?" asked the friend. "Surely if you've seen Juan, you've seen Amal."

• •

A woman lion tamer had the big cats under such control they took a lump of sugar from her lips. "Anyone can do that!" a skeptic yelled. The ringmaster came over and asked, "Would you like to try it?" "Sure" replied the man, "but first get those crazy lions out of there."

• •

A priest who considered that he had lived a godly life on earth, was upset to get to heaven and find himself shackled to an ugly, nasty woman. Then he spotted a former bishop chained to a young woman, who, in her lifetime, had been renowned for her beauty and charm.

The priest went to St. Peter to complain. "It's none of your business," said St. Peter. "You get on with your penance and let her get on with hers."

• •

Late one night after an evening of carousing, Smitty took a shortcut through the graveyard and stumbled into a newly dug grave. He couldn't get out so he lay at the bottom and fell asleep. Early next morning the old caretaker heard moans and groans coming from deep in the earth and he went over to investigate. He saw the shivering figure at the bottom and demanded. "What's wrong with ya that you're making all that noise?" "I'm awful cold" came the response. "Well, it's no wonder," said the caretaker. "You've gone and kicked all the dirt off ya."

☻ A man was told by his doctor that he only had six months to live. "Doc," he said, "is there anything I can do?" "Yes" replied the doctor. "First give all your money to the poor. Next, move to a cold-water shack in the backwoods and marry a woman with six young children." "Will this give me more time?" he asked. "No - but it'll be the longest six months of your life."

☻ Too busy to break away from his work, a radio DJ and his bride held their wedding ceremony in the second-floor conference room over his office. So many fans showed up that the building collapsed. There's a moral to this story:
Never marry above your station.

☻ Stock Market advice: It's not the bulls and bears you have to watch out for - it's the bum steers.

☻ A student of English was sent to prison as a first offender and was advised by a longtime inmate that if he made amorous advances to the warden's wife, she'd get him released quickly. "But I can't do that," the student protested. It's wrong to end a sentence with a proposition."

☻ Tell your boss what you really think of him - and the truth shall set you free.

☻ All men make mistakes, but married men find out about them sooner.

VERSE IN A DELI WINDOW:
"We do not make a stingy sandwich
We pile the cold cuts high.
Our customers will see salami
Coming through the rye."

😊 Two kids were trying to figure out what game to play. The little boy said "Let's play doctor." "Okay" said the little girl. "You operate and I'll sue."

"Betcha can't guess how old I am," said the elderly gentleman to a group of ladies in the lounge of the old folks home. "Bet I can" said one of the ladies. "Take off all your clothes right now and run across this room and I'll tell you exactly how old you are. Never one to lose a bet, the elderly gentleman did as he was told and came back for her answer. "You're 91 years old," she said. "That's absolutely right. How on earth could you tell that?" he asked. "You told me yesterday" she replied.

😊 Clothes don't necessarily make the man, but a good suit makes a lawyer.

Ever get the feeling that you're cutting the lawn of life with cuticle scissors?

😊 A certain parrot was quite often blurting out profanity. Exasperated, his new owner warns him, "One more word of profanity and you go in the refrigerator." The parrot says, "Damn!" With that, the owner tosses him into the refrigerator. Getting used to the darkness after a while, the parrot sees a dressed chicken and says "all I said was damn, what the devil did you say?"

😊 "With a single stroke of a brush," said the art teacher, "Joshua Reynolds could change a smiling face into a frowning one." "That's nothing," said one small boy. "So can my mother."

"I think that I shall never see a billboard lovely as a tree.
Perhaps, unless the billboards fall, I'll never see a tree at all."

Ogden Nash

Time Honored Truths

*Don't sweat the petty things, and don't pet the
sweaty things.*

One tequila, two tequila, three tequila floor.

*One nice thing about egotists:
They don't talk about other people.*

*To be intoxicated is to feel sophisticated
but not be able to say it.*

*Never underestimate the power of stupid
people in large groups.*

Age is a very high price to pay for maturity

Women like silent men.... they think they're listening.

*Give a man a fish and he will eat for a day. Teach him to
fish and he will sit in a boat and drink beer all day.*

A fool and his money are soon partying.

☺ Reaching the end of a job interview, the Human Resources person asked a young engineer fresh out of MIT, "And what starting salary were you looking for?"

The engineer replied, "In the neighborhood of $125,000 a year, depending on the benefits package."

The interviewer said, "Well, what would you say to a package of 5 weeks vacation, 14 paid holidays, full medical and dental benefits, company matching retirement fund to 50% of salary and a company car leased every 2 years - say a red corvette?"

The engineer sat up straight and said, "Wow! Are you kidding?"

The interviewer replied, "Yeah, but you started it."

☺ A sign on a bulletin board of a church down the street announced the topic for Sunday's sermon: "Do You Know What Hell Is?" Underneath someone had scribbled "Come and hear our organist."

Policeman: I have to give you a ticket, Ma'am. You were traveling sixty miles an hour!

Lady: Impossible, I've only been driving for twenty minutes.

Old accountants never die — they just lose their balance.

- Never fall in love with a tennis player. To him, "love" means nothing.

- Some say that no person should keep too much to oneself. Revenue Canada is of the same opinion.

- A visitor to the farm of a country cousin was inspecting a vicious-looking bull and called to the farmer "Hey, is this bull safe?" "Yep," replied the farmer. "He's a lot safer than you are."

- You never know what a poor loser you are until you try dieting.

- Many people are willing to meet the other guy halfway; trouble is, most people are a pretty poor judge of distance!"

- The behaviour of some children suggests that their parents embarked on the sea of matrimony without a paddle.

- A bachelor is lucky - he can make a mistake and never know it.

- Somehow it just doesn't seem right to go over the river and through the woods to Grandmother's condo.

- A road map will tell us everything we want to know except how to fold it up again.

- The passing years make youngsters ponder. Why Dad gets grayer and Mom gets blonder.

THE PURCHASE

A farmer had been taken several times by the local car dealer. One day, the car dealer informed the farmer that he was coming over to purchase a cow. The farmer priced his unit as follows:

BASIC COW	**$499.95**
Shipping & Handling	**35.75**
Extra Stomach	**79.25**
Two-tone exterior	**142.10**
Produce storage compartment	**126.50**
Heavy duty straw chopper	**189.60**
Four-spigot/high-output drain system	**149.20**
Automatic fly swatter	**88.50**
Genuine cowhide upholstery	**179.90**
Deluxe dual horns	**59.25**
Automatic fertilizer attachment	**339.40**
4 x 4 traction drive assembly	**884.16**
Pre-delivery wash and comb	**69.80**
Farmer's Suggested List Price	**$2,843.36**
Additional dealer adjustment............................	**300.00**
TOTAL LIST PRICE (including options)	**$3,143.36**

REMEMBER... a kick in the behind is really a step forward.

☺ Of all the things you wear, your expression is the most important.

Childhood: That time of life when you make funny faces in the mirror.

Middle Age: That time of life when the mirror gets even.

☺ It's not the pace of life that concerns me - it's the sudden stop at the end!

☺ The trouble with self-made men is that they usually worship their creator.

☺ Beware of the man who says he enjoys a cold shower in the morning - he'll also lie about other things!

☺ Old politicians never die - they just become devoted.

☺ The trouble with using experience as a guide is that the final exam comes first and then the lesson.

☺ The reason lightning doesn't strike twice in the same place is that the same place isn't there the second time!

☺ Have you ever considered that if it weren't for the last minute, nothing would ever get done?"

**It's the little things that bother us
and put us on a rack.
You can sit upon a mountain,
But not upon a tack!**

Chuckles

An insurance agent was writing a policy for a cowboy. "Ever had an accident?" he asked. "Nope" the cowboy replied "But I've been bit by a rattlesnake and kicked by a bronco." "Don't you call those accidents?" the agent asked. "Nope" said the cowboy, "the critters did it on purpose!"

A Protestant felt too guilty about his sin of stealing to tell his own pastor, so he went to a Catholic priest to confess.

"I have been stealing lumber from the local lumberyard for ten years," the man confided to the priest. "Well, my son," said the priest, "we must talk about restitution."

"Anything you say!" replied the sinner.

"How much lumber do you suppose you have stolen through the years? Five hundred dollars worth? A thousand dollars worth? Two thousand dollars worth?"

"Oh, more than that," answered the thief. "Do you want to make a Novena?" the priest asked. The fellow cocked his head and said "Father, if you've got the plans for it, I've got the lumber."

😊 It's ok to let your mind go blank - just as long as you remember to turn off the sound!

😊 Hear about the hummingbird and door bell that fell in love, got married, and had a little humdinger?

😊 If lawyers are disbarred and clergymen defrocked, doesn't it follow that electrician's can be delighted; musicians denoted; cowboys deranged; models deposed; tree surgeons debarked and dry cleaners depressed?

ABOUT DIETS:

I'm on a seafood diet. I see food and I eat it.

☺ The two biggest sellers in any bookstore are the cookbooks and the diet books. The cookbooks tell you how to prepare the food and the diet books tell you how not to eat any of it.

☺ Eat as much food as you want. Just don't swallow it.

☺ I'm allergic to chocolate. When I eat it I break out in fat.

☺ The second day of a diet is always easier than the first. By the second day you're off it.

☺ You can see why America is called a melting pot - everybody's dieting.

☺ I took up riding horses as part of my diet program - in two weeks the horse lost eighteen pounds.

☺ I went on a diet that allowed me to drink wine and eat vegetables. In ten days I lost five pounds and my driver's license.

☺ Diets are for people who are thick and tired of it.

☺ I went on a drinking man's diet once. In three weeks I lost twenty-one days.

☺ I know a woman who lived on coconuts and milk to lose weight. She still weighs the same but boy can she climb trees!

Chuckles

QUOTES FROM A COLLECTION OF LETTERS WHICH WERE ACTUALLY RECEIVED BY LANDLORDS FROM THEIR TENANTS.

"I wish to complain that my father hurt his ankle very badly when he put his foot in the hole in his back passage."

"This is to let you know that there is a smell coming from the man next door.'

"The toilet seat is cracked. Where do I stand."

"I am writing on behalf of my sink, which is running away from the wall."

"Our toilet is blocked and we cannot bath the children until it is cleared."

"Will you please send a man to look at my water. It is a funny colour and not fit to drink."

"Please send someone to fix our bath tap. My wife got her toe stuck in it and it is very uncomfortable for both of us."

TRAVEL TIP:
The longer you drive,
the better your
bug collection.

Jock hurries into a pub in Scotland; runs up to Angus and asks: "The bonnie Great Dane doggie tied up outside - is he not yours, Angus" "Aye" answers Angus.

"Well hoot man, I'm afraid my wee doggie may have killed him."

"Oh, noooo" chuckles Angus, "you're mistaken Jock. What kind of doggie could kill my bonnie Great Dane?"

"My Chihuahua, Angus. I think the wee fellow got stuck in his throat."

A highly inebriated fellow called the fire station:
"Come quick, my house is on fire."
Fire fighter: "Right away - how do we get there?"
Caller: "Don't you still have your little red truck?"

😊 There is never enough time, unless you're serving it.

😊 A disgusted wife was standing at the door watching her husband stagger up the front path. Wife: "Drunk again!" Husband: "Me too."

😊 What do you call a sleep-walking Nun?" A Roamin' Catholic.

😊 Kissing a feller with a beard is like a picnic. You don't mind going through a light brush to get there.

😊 Uncle Nabob takes a drink every now and then to steady his nerves. He gets pretty steady. Sometimes he don't move at all.

Chuckles

- Never judge a dog's pedigree by the kinds of books he chews!

- There was once a lovely young woman named Carmen Gowen. Her family called her Carmen and her teacher called her Gowen. This caused her so much confusion that by the time she was 16 years old she still didn't know whether she was Carmen or Gowen.

- Hear about the dentist who married a manicurist? They fought tooth and nail.

- Ideas are very much like children–your own are wonderful.

(HONEST TO GOODNESS) CHURCH ANNOUNCEMENTS !

"For those of you who have children and don't know it; we have a nursery downstairs."

"Remember in prayer the many who are sick of our church and community."

Don't let worry kill you off...let the church help."

"Our mixed chorus sang last Sunday in a regional broadcast from Winnipeg. It was nice to hear them and realize they were nearly a thousand miles away."

☺ Do you know how many divorced men it takes to change a lightbulb?
None - they never get the house.

☺ Know the fastest way to trace your family tree?
Run for public office.

☺ How many men does it take to change a roll of toilet paper?
Don't know - it's never happened.

☺ What's the definition of an optimist?
An accordion player with a beeper.

An Irish, a British and a Scottish clergyman were discussing their methods of determining how much of the weekly collection they allocate to salary and parish expenses and how much each of them send to church headquarters for missionaries and outreach.

The Irishman explained that there was a line painted down the center aisle of his church and standing over it, he tossed the week's collection up in the air. "What comes down on the right of the line belongs to the Lord and the rest I keep," said he.

The Englishman then offered his technique. "I use the altar rail in much the same way" he said, "and what comes down on the altar side goes to the mother church for the Lord's work and the balance I keep for the parish salaries and upkeep."

The Scotsman looked askance at the two of them. "My system is much simpler" he advised. "I too toss the weekly collection into the air - and I figure that what stays up is God's and what comes down is mine."

😊 Have you heard about the symphony conductor with more engagements than he could shake a stick at?

😊 Hear about the politician who retired from public service due to ill health? The voters got sick of him.

😊 A man noticed that a blood vessel on his forehead would enlarge as the barometric pressure fell. He learned to predict storms by observing his weather vein.

😊 A four year old little girl went to the animal shelter with her class to see a new litter of kittens. Upon returning home she excitedly informed her mother that they saw two boy kittens and two girl kittens. "How did you know that?" asked her mother. "Teacher picked them up and looked underneath" she replied. "I think it's printed on the bottom."

😊 A veterinarian quit his practice and successfully ran for the legislature. One day, in the middle of a heated debate, his opponent asked with a sneer: "Is it true that you're an animal doctor?" "Indeed it is," replied the veterinarian. "Are you ill?"

😊 Bulls cannot distinguish red from any other colour. They are, in fact, colour blind. What makes them angry enough to charge is simply that they deeply resent matadors calling this visual weakness to their attention and to the attention of thousands of spectators.

😊 Said the circus manager to the human cannonball: "You can't quit! Where will I find another man of your caliber?"

Fashion:
Something that goes in one year
and out the other.

WHY IS IT THAT ? ? ? ?

- Some people have a great frame of mind and no picture.

- Nobody who can read is ever successful at cleaning out an attic.

- Store clerks usually follow the line of least assistance.

- Many small boys are the kind of kids their mothers wouldn't let them play with.

- A bath mat is a little rug that children like to stand beside.

- Forbidden fruit is supposed to taste sweeter but it usually spoils faster.

- The most efficient labour saving device is still money.

- There is nothing more satisfying than seeing your children have teenagers of their own.

- The only way you can borrow money from a bank is to present sufficient evidence that you don't need it.

- If you want to see a short winter, borrow some money that's due in the spring.

- No matter how crowded the party, there's always room for one bore.

● People are like little tea bags. They don't know their own strength until they get into hot water.

● Hear about the two accountants who fell in love. The attraction was purely fiscal!

● Why aren't plumbers' assistants called drainees?

● Politicians and diapers should be changed frequently and for the same reason.

An accountant was hiking in the country when he came upon a shepherd tending a large flock of sheep. The accountant was quite taken with the scene of the sheep on the hillside and asked the shepherd, "If I can guess how many sheep you are tending, may I keep one?" The shepherd figured there wasn't much chance of the fellow guessing correctly so he agreed.

"You are tending exactly 173 sheep," the accountant announced. The shepherd was astonished, since that was the exact number of sheep in his flock.

"May I pick out my sheep now?" asked the accountant. The shepherd unhappily agreed. After much contemplation, the accountant selected one and slung it over his shoulders to carry home. The shepherd had a thought. "If I guess your occupation" he said, "can I have my sheep back?" The accountant figured there was little chance of the shepherd guessing what he did so he agreed. "You're an accountant," said the shepherd.

Amazed, the accountant asked, "How did you know?"

The shepherd replied "Put the dog down and we'll talk about it."

ADVERTISING BLOOPERS

Lost: Small apricot poodle. Reward.
Neutered. Like one of the family.

Lost: Beagle, partly blind, hard of
hearing, castrated, answers to
the name of Lucky.

DINNER SPECIAL
     Turkey $2.35:
     Chicken or Beef $2.25;
     Children $2.00.

For sale: An antique desk.
Suitable for lady - with thick legs and large drawers.

Four-poster bed: 101 years old. Perfect for antique lover.

Now is your chance to have your ears pierced and get an extra
pair to take home as well.

Ears pierced while you wait.

Our experienced Mom will care for your child.
Fenced yard, meals and smacks included.

For Sale: Eight puppies from a German Shepherd and an
Alaskan Hussy.

Dog for Sale: Eats anything; especially fond of children.

Chuckles

A goat was nosing around the rubbish dump when it found a reel of film. It sniffed at it, licked at it and then quickly gobbled it up. Another goat came along. "Was that film any good?" he asked. "It was okay," replied the first goat, "But I preferred the book."

CLERICAL ERROR: The ministers' conference was concluding when one pastor was requested to give a lot of thanks to wives holding the fort at home.

"Having enjoyed this spiritual feast" he said, "I cannot help being filled with gratitude for the work of my own wife, back at my church, bravely carrying on with the deacons."

ACTUAL NEWSPAPER HEADLINES

"Grandmother of Eight Makes Hole in One"

"Deaf Mute Gets New Hearing in Killing"

"Two Convicts Evade Noose, Jury Hung"

"Stiff Opposition Expected to Casketless Funeral plan"

"Experts Say School Bus Passengers Should Be Belted"

"Police Begin Campaign to Run Down Jaywalkers"

"Iraqi Head Seeks Arms"

"Quarter of a Million Chinese Live on Water"

An old farmer in Maine was plowing his cornfield with his mule when one of the rings on his plow chain came off. He hunted high and low but couldn't find it so he un-hitched the mule from the plow, climbed up on its back and headed off to a country store he knew about, five or six miles down the road. After a short while a friend of his in a car happened along. He pulled up beside the mule and asked if his friend wanted a ride.

"Shore!" " said the farmer. "I'm a-goin' down to the General Store to try and buy me an open ring for my plow chain. You goin' that far?" The driver said he was and would be glad to give him a lift. "But what about your mule?" the driver asked. "Aw, don't worry none about him. He'll keep up, gist running along a-hind us."

So down the road they drove, with the old mule running along behind them. The driver looked down at the speedometer. "We're only doing twenty five," he said. "And your mule is keeping up just fine."

"Aw, he can go faster than that" the farmer said. "He'll keep up." So the driver upped his speed to thirty-five. He looked in the rear view mirror and the old mule was right behind him, keeping up just fine.

"Aw, he can go faster than that," the farmer said. "He'll keep up." "We'll see about that", the driver said to himself and upped his speed to 45. The old mule stayed right behind him. The driver kind of smiled to himself and really stepped on the gas. The speed shot up to 65. Again he looked in the read view mirror and the old mule was right behind him, but looked strange.

"Say," said the driver, "your mule is keeping up, but he looks funny. His eyes are bulged out and he's got his tongue sticking out," he said.

"Which side of the mouth is his tongue stickin' out of?" asked the farmer.

"Why, it's the left side" the driver replied.

"Well, don't change lanes," said the farmer. "He's gettin' ready to pass you.!"

MODERN PHILOSOPHIES

- A conclusion is the place at which you get tired of thinking.

- Experience is something you don't get until just after you need it.

- The sooner you fall behind, the more time you'll have to catch up.

- He who hesitates is probably right.

- No one is listening until you make a mistake.

- Monday is an awful way to spend 1/7th of your life.

- The colder the X-ray table, the more of your body is required on it.

- The hardness of the butter is proportional to the softness of the bread.

- To steal ideas from one person is plagiarism; to steal from many is research.

- The problem with the gene pool is that there is no lifeguard.

- You never learn to swear until you learn to drive.

FACTS OF LIFE

☺ The two most common elements in the universe are hydrogen and stupidity.

☺ If at first you don't succeed, skydiving is not for you.

☺ Nothing in the universe travels faster than a bad cheque.

☺ It has recently been discovered that research causes cancer in rats.

☺ The trouble with doing something right the first time is that nobody appreciates how difficult it was.

☺ Clothes make the person. Naked people have little or no influence on society.

☺ Vital papers will demonstrate their vitality by moving from where you left them to where you can't find them.

☺ Law of Probability Dispersal:
Whatever it is that hits the fan will not be evenly distributed.

☺ The only job where you start at the top is digging a hole.

As one caveman said to the other:
"You figure it out. Everything we eat is 100% natural yet our life expectancy is only 27 years."

HAVE YOU EVER WONDERED?

If olive oil comes from olives,
where does baby oil come from?

Why does your nose run, and your feet smell?

How much deeper would the ocean be
if sponges didn't live there?

Did George Washington just
flash a quarter for his ID?

Why isn't there mouse-flavoured
cat food?

How can there be self-help groups?

Why are there interstate highways in Hawaii?

Why is it that when you transport something by
car, it's called a shipment,
but when you transport something by ship,
it's called a cargo?

Why do we play in recitals and recite in plays?

Why isn't phonetic spelled the way it sounds?

If knees were backwards,
what would chairs look like?

Daffy-nitions

Cannibal: Someone who is fed up with people.

Chickens: The only animals you eat before they are born and after they are dead.

Committee: A body that keeps minutes and wastes hours.

Dust: Mud with the juice squeezed out.

Gossip: A person who will never tell a lie if the truth will do more damage.

Handkerchief: Cold storage.

Inflation: Cutting money in half without damaging the paper.

Myth: A female moth.

Mosquito: An insect that makes you like flies better.

Toothache: The pain that drives you to extraction.

Yawn: An honest opinion openly expressed.

One night, a Delta twin-engine puddle jumper was flying somewhere above New Jersey. There were five people on board: the pilot, Michael Jordan, Bill Gates, the Dali Lama and a hippie.

Suddenly an illegal oxygen generator exploded loudly in the luggage compartment and the passenger cabin began to fill with smoke. The cockpit door opened and the pilot burst into the compartment.

"Gentlemen," he began, "I have good news and bad news. The bad news is that we're about to crash in New Jersey. The good news is that there are four parachutes and I have one of them!" With that the pilot threw open the door and jumped from the plane.

Michael Jordan was on his feet in a flash. "Gentlemen," he said, "I am the world's greatest athlete. The world needs great athletes. I think the world's greatest athlete should have a parachute!" With these words, he grabbed one of the remaining parachutes and hurtled through the door and into the night.

Bill Gates rose and said 'Gentlemen, I am the world's smartest man. The world needs smart men. I think the world's smartest man should have a parachute too." He grabbed one and out he jumped.

The Dali Lama spoke. "My son" he said "I have lived a satisfying life and have known the bliss of True Enlightenment. You have your life ahead of you; you take a parachute and I will go down with the plane."

The hippie smiled slowly and said "Hey, don't worry, pop. The world's smartest man just jumped out wearing my backpack."

😊 There's a guy with a Doberman Pinscher and a guy with a Chihuahua. The guy with the Doberman Pinscher says to the guy with a Chihuahua. "Let's go over to that restaurant and get something to eat."

The guys with the Chihuahua says "We can't go in there. We've got dogs with us." The guy with the Doberman Pinscher says "Just follow my lead."

They walk over to the restaurant, the guy with the Doberman puts on a pair of dark glasses and he starts to walk in. A fellow at the door says "Sorry mac, no pets allowed." The guy with the Doberman says "You don't understand. This is my seeing-eye dog."

The fellow at the door says "A Doberman Pinscher?" The guy says "Yes, they're using them now, they're very good."

The fellow at the door says "Come on in." The guy with the Chihuahua figures, "What the heck" so he puts on a pair of dark glasses and starts to walk in. The fellow at he door says, "Sorry pal, no pets allowed." The guy with the Chihuahua says, "You don't understand. This is my seeing-eye dog."

The fellow at the door says "A Chihuahua?"

The guy with the Chihuahua says "You mean they gave me a Chihuahua?"

😊 Two cannibals were walking through the jungle talking when the first mentioned to the second that he had a bellyache.

The second cannibal asked, "Well did you eat anything out of the ordinary lately?" "No" replied the first, "All I've eaten recently was a missionary and he wasn't too good." "Hmm" said the second, "and how did you cook him?" "I boiled him as usual," replied the first.

The second asked, "Was he tall, thin and wearing a black robe with a white collar?" "No" replied the first, "He was short, fat, balding and wore a brown robe."

"Aha" exclaimed the second. "There's your problem, you shouldn't have boiled him. That was a Friar!"

PARENTAL DEFINITIONS

Dumbwaiter: One who asks if the kids would care to order dessert.

Feedback: The inevitable result when your baby doesn't appreciate the stringed carrots.

Hearsay: What toddlers do when anyone mutters a dirty word.

Impregnable: A woman whose memory of labor is still vivid.

Top Bunk: Where you should never put a child in Superman pyjamas.

Family Planning: The art of spacing your children the proper distance apart to keep you on the edge of financial disaster.

Full Name: What you call your child when you're mad at him.

Grandparents: The people who think your children are wonderful even though they're sure you're not raising them right.

OW: The first word spoken by children with siblings.

Puddle: A small body of water that draws other small bodies wearing dry shoes into it.

☻ There was once a very inspirational preacher, but he had a tremendous weakness for golf. Every chance he got, he was found on the golf course swinging away. It was an obsession for him.

One Sunday was a picture perfect day for golfing. The sun was out, no clouds in the sky and the temperature was just right. The preacher was in a quandary as to what to do and very shortly the urge to play golf overcame him.

He called an assistant to tell him that he was sick and could not conduct the service that morning, put his clubs in the car and drove three hours to a golf course where no one would recognize him. Happily, he began to play the course.

An angel up above was watching the preacher and was quite perturbed. She went to God and said, "Look at the preacher. He should be punished for what he is doing." God nodded in agreement.

The preacher teed up on the first hole. He swung at the ball and it sailed effortlessly through the air and landed right in the cup three hundred and fifty yards away. Wow! A picture perfect hole-in-one. He was amazed and ecstatic.

The angel was a little shocked. She turned to God and said "Begging Your pardon, but I thought we were agreed that he should be punished?"

The Lord smiled and said "Think about it - who can he tell?"

Chuckles

THE STORY OF CREATION - IN TODAY'S WORLD!

In the beginning God created Heaven and Earth. Quickly he was faced with a class action suit for failure to file an environmental impact statement. He was granted a temporary permit for the project, but was stymied with the Cease and Desist order for the early part.

Appearing at the hearing, God was asked why he began his earthly project in the first place. He replied that he just liked to be creative.

Then God said "Let there be light." Officials immediately demanded to know how the light would be made. Would there be strip mining? What about thermal pollution? God explained that the light would come from a huge ball of fire. God was granted provisional permission to make light, assuming that no smoke would result from the ball of fire; that he would obtain a building permit and (to conserve energy) would have the light out half the time. God agreed and said he would call the light "Day" and the darkness "Night". Officials replied that they were not interested in semantics.

God said "Let the earth bring forth green herbs and such as many seed." The Environmental Protection Agency agreed, so long as native seed was used.

Then God said "Let waters bring forth creeping creatures having life; and the fowl that may fly over the earth." Officials pointed out this would require approval from the Department of Game coordinated with the Heavenly Wildlife Federation and the Audubongelic Society.

Everything was ok until God said he wanted to complete the project in six days. Officials informed him it would take at least 200 days to review the application and the environmental impact statement. After that there would be a public hearing. Then there would be 10-12 months before........

At this point, God created Hell!

HAVE YOU EVER WONDERED?

When your pet bird sees you reading the newspaper, does he wonder why you're just sitting there staring at the carpeting?

If an orange is called an "Orange", why isn't a lime called a "Green" or a lemon called a "Yellow" ?

What are Preparations A through H?

After eating, do amphibians have to wait one hour before getting out of the water?

If a man is standing in the middle of the forest, speaking, and there is no woman around to hear him - is he still wrong?

If a deaf person swears, does his mother wash his hands with soap?

If someone with multiple personalities threatens to kill himself, is it considered a hostage situation?

Is there another word for synonym?

When sign makers go on strike, is anything written on their signs?

When you open a bag of cotton balls, is the top one meant to be thrown away?

Where do forest rangers go to "get away from it all?"

What do you do when you see an endangered animal eating an endangered plant?

Chuckles

A fellow goes into a bar and sees a beautiful woman sitting at the bar. After an hour of gathering up his courage he finally goes over to her and asks, tentatively, "Um, would you mind if I chatted with you for a while?" To which she responds by yelling at the top of her lungs, "No, I won't sleep with you tonight!"

Everyone at the bar is now staring at them. Naturally the guy is hopelessly and completely embarrassed and he slinks back to his table. After a few minutes the woman walks over to him and apologizes. She says "I'm sorry if I embarrassed you. You see, I'm a graduate student in psychology and I'm studying how people respond to embarrassing situations.

To which he responds, at the top of his lungs, "What do you mean $200."

Following a fine night on the town, a drunk decides to go ice fishing so he gathers his gear and goes walking around until he finds a big patch of ice. He heads into the center of the ice and begins to saw a hole. All of a sudden a loud booming voice comes out of the sky.

"You will find no fish under that ice." The drunk looks around but sees no one. He starts sawing again. Once more the voice speaks, "There are no fish under the ice."

The drunk looks all around but can't see a single soul. He picks up the saw and tries one more time to finish. Before he can even start cutting, the huge voice interrupts "I have warned you three times now. There are no fish!"

The drunk is flustered and somewhat scared, so he asks the voice, "How do you know there are no fish? Are you God trying to warn me?"

"No" the voice booms forth, "I am the manager of this hockey rink."

Two nuns are travelling through Europe in their car. They get to Transylvania and are stopped at a traffic light. Suddenly, a diminutive Dracula jumps onto the hood of the car and hisses through the windshield.

"Quick, quick!" shouts the first nun, "What shall I do?"

"Turn the windshield wipers on, that will get rid of the abomination," says the second.

She switches them on, knocking Dracula about, but he clings on and hisses again at the nuns.

"What shall I do now?" shouts the first nun. "Switch on the windshield washer. I filled it up with Holy Water at the Vatican" says the second.

Dracula steams as the water burns him, but he clings on and hisses again at the nuns.

"Now what?" shouts the first nun. "Show him your cross" says the second.

Whereupon the driver winds down her window and shouts "GET THE HELL OFF MY BLOODY HOOD".

 BUMPER STICKERS:

Change is inevitable, except from a vending machine.

Where there's a will - I want to be in it!

Chuckles

A neutron goes into a bar and asks the bartender, "How much for a beer?" The bartender replies, "For you, no charge."

Two boll weevils grew up in South Carolina. One went to Hollywood and became a famous actor. The other stayed behind in the cotton fields and never amounted to much. The second one naturally became known as the lesser of two weevils.

Did you hear about the buddhist who refused his dentist's novocaine during root canal work? He wanted to transcend dental medication.

A middle-aged woman had a heart attack and was taken to the hospital. While on the operating table she had a near-death experience. During that experience she saw God and asked if this was it. God said no, and explained that she had another 30 to 40 years to live.

Upon her recovery she decided to just stay in the hospital and have a face lift, liposuction, breast augmentation and a tummy tuck. She even had someone come in and change her hair colour. She figured since she had another 30 to 40 years, she might as well make the most of it.

She walked out of the hospital after the last operation and was killed by an ambulance speeding up to the hospital. She arrived in front of God again and asked, "I thought you said I had another 30 to 40 years to live?"

God replied, "I didn't recognize you."

A man was sitting at a bar enjoying an after-work cocktail when an exceptionally gorgeous and voluptuous young woman entered. She was so striking that the man could not take his eyes away from her.

The young woman noticed his overly attentive stare and walked directly toward him. Before he could offer his apologies for being so rude, the young woman said to him, "I'll do anything, absolutely anything that you want me to do, no matter how strange, for $100 - but there's one condition." Flabbergasted, the man asked what the condition was.

She replied "You have to tell me what you want me to do in just three words."

The man considered her proposition for a moment, withdrew his wallet from his pocket and slowly counted out five $20 bills, which he pressed into the young woman's hand. He looked deeply into her eyes and slowly, meaningfully said: "Paint my house."

BUMPER STICKERS:

**Back up my hard drive?
How do I put it in reverse?**

**Everyone has a photographic memory.
Some just don't have film.**

**When the chips are down,
the buffalo is empty.**

**She's always late. Her ancestors
arrived on the June Flower.**

**Despite the cost of living, have you noticed
how it remains so popular?**

THE ALL-NEW DICTIONARY
OF FRACTURED MEDICAL TERMS

Barium -What you do when the patient dies.

Urine - The opposite of "You're out."

Cauterize - Made eye contact with her.

Ova - Finished, done.

Sperm - To reject.

Dilate - To live a long time.

Enema - Opposite of friend.

Node - Was aware of.

Fibrillate - To tell a small lie.

D & C - Where Washington is.

Rectum - Dang near killed 'em.

Paradox - Two doctors

Coronary - Yellow bird

Constipation - Endangered feces.

Penis - Guy who plays the piano

Humerus - Tell us what we want to hear.

Intestine - Currently taking an exam.

Genital - Non-Jewish patient.

Sacrum - Holy

Papsmear - To slander your father

Seizure - Roman Emperor

White count - The number of caucasians.

AFTERTHOUGHT:
Isn't it a bit unnerving that what doctors do they call "practice"???

Chuckles

A group of chess enthusiasts checked into a hotel and were standing in the lobby discussing their recent tournament victories.

After about an hour, the manager came out of the office and asked them to disperse.

"But why?" they asked, as they moved off.

"Because," he replied. "I can't stand chess nuts boasting in an open foyer."

A mother was teaching her 3 year old daughter the Lord's prayer. For several evenings at bedtime she repeated it after her mother. One night she said she was ready to solo.

The mother listened with pride as she carefully enunciated each word right up to the end. "Lead us not into temptation," she prayed, "but deliver us some E-mail. Amen."

During a routine checkup, a dentist asked his patient if he had been eating any different foods lately.

The man replied that yes, his wife had learned to make a wonderful hollandaise sauce and he'd been eating it on just about everything.

"Well" the dentist said "I think the acidity in the sauce's lemon juice is eroding your denture plate. I'll make you a new one, but this time I'll make it out of chrome."

"Chrome" the patient asked. "Why chrome?"

"Because" the dentist replied "everyone knows there's no plate like chrome for the hollandaise."

Little Ricky opened a large family Bible and gazed in awe at a dried, pressed leaf. "Look" he said in a hushed voice. "Adam's suit."

- The New Official Language -

The European Commission has just announced an agreement whereby English will be the official language of the European Union, rather than German, which was the other possibility.

Year 1 - "s" will replace the soft "c". This will sertainly make the sivil servants jump for joy. The hard "c" will be dropped in favour of the "k". This will klear up konfusion and keyboards kan have 1 less key/letter.

Year 2 - There will be growing publik enthusiasm this year when the troublesome "ph" will be replaced by "f", which will make words like FOTOGRAF 20% shorter.

Year 3 - Publik akseptanse of the new spelling kan be expekted to reach the stage where more komplikated changes are possible. Governments will enkourage the removal of the double letters which have always ben a deterent to akurate speling. Also we al wil agre that the horible mes of the silent "e" in the language is disgrasful and they should go away.

Year 4 - Peopl wil be reseptiv to steps such as replasing "th" with "z" and "w" with "v".

Year 5 - During ze fifz year z unesesary "o" kan be dropd from vords kontaining "ou" and similar changes vud of kors be aplid to ozer kombinations of leters. After ziz fifz yer, v vil have a reli sensible riten styl. Zer vil be no mor trubls or difikultis and evrivun vil find it ezi tu understand ech ozer.

ZE DREM VIL FINALI KOM TRU!

Chuckles

An American soldier had just returned from several weeks of intense action on the front lines. He had been granted R&R and made it to Southhampton, England, there to board a train for a few days in London.

The train was very crowded, so the soldier walked the length of it looking for an empty seat. The only seat unoccupied was directly across from a well dressed middle aged lady and was being used by her little dog.

The war weary soldier asked "Please ma'am, may I sit in that seat?" The English woman looked down her nose at the soldier, sniffed, and said, "You Americans, you are such a rude class of people. Can't you see my little Fifi is using that seat?"

The soldier walked away, determined to find a place to rest, but after another trip down to the end of the train, found himself again facing the woman with the dog in the opposite seat.

Again he asked "Please, lady. Can I sit there, I'm very tired." The English woman wrinkled her nose and snorted, "You Americans. Not only are you rude, you are also very inconsiderate."

The soldier didn't say anything else; he leaned over, picked up the little dog and tossed it out the window of the train and sat down in the empty seat.

An English gentleman, sitting across the aisle said, "You know, sir, you Americans do seem to have a penchant for doing the wrong thing. You eat holding the fork in the wrong hand. You drive your autos on the wrong side of the road. And now, sir, you have thrown the wrong bitch out of the window."

GET INFECTED!

Smiling is infectious. You catch it like the flu
When someone smiled at me today,
I started smiling too!
I passed around the corner and someone saw my grin.
When he smiled I realized I'd passed it on to him.
I thought about that smile then I realized its worth.
A single smile, just like mine, could travel round the earth.
So, if you feel a smile begin, don't leave it undetected.
Let's start an epidemic and get the world infected!

Sherlock Holmes and Dr. Watson went on a camping trip. After a good meal and a bottle of wine they lay down for the night and went to sleep.

Some hours later Holmes awoke and nudged his faithful friend. "Watson, look up at the sky and tell me what you see." Watson replied, "I see millions and millions of stars." "What does that tell you?" asked Holmes.

Watson pondered for a minute and replied, "Astronomically, it tells me that there are millions of galaxies and potentially billions of planets. Astrologically, I observe that Saturn is in Leo. Horologically, I deduce that the time is approximately a quarter past three. Theologically, I can see that God is all powerful and that we are small and insignificant. Meteorologically, I suspect that we will have a clear and sunny day tomorrow. What does it tell you, Holmes?"

Holmes was silent for a minute, then spoke: "Watson, you idiot. Somebody has stolen our tent."

(MORE) CHURCH NOTICE BLOOPERS

"Scouts are saving aluminum cans, bottles, and other items to be recycled. Proceeds will be used to cripple children."

"Ushers will eat latecomers."

"The Ladies Bible Study will be held Thursday morning at 10. All ladies are invited to lunch in the Fellowship Hall after the B.S. is done."

"The Pastor would appreciate it if the ladies of the congregation would lend him their electric girdles for the pancake breakfast next Sunday morning."

"Low Self-Esteem Support Group will meet Thursday at 7 to 8:30 p.m. Please use the back door."

"Pastor is on vacation. Massages can be given to the church secretary."

"The third verse of Blessed Assurance will be sung without musical accomplishment."

"The Rev. Merriwether spoke briefly, much to the delight of the audience."

"The Pastor will preach his farewell message, after which the choir will sing "Break Forth Into Joy".

"Remember in prayer the many who are sick of our church and community."

"A song fest was hell at the Methodist church on Wednesday."

"Today's Sermon: How Much Can a Man Drink? with hymns from a full choir."

Seen on a Church Bulletin Board during the minister's illness: "God is good - Dr. Hargreaves
is better."

"Potluck supper: Prayer and medication to follow."

"The choir invites any member of the congregation who enjoys sinning to join the choir."

HISTORY OF MEDICINE

The Year	The Cure
2000 B.C.	Here, eat this root.
1000 A.D.	That root is heathen.
	Here, say this prayer.
1850 A.D.	That prayer is superstition.
	Here, drink this potion
1940 A.D.	That potion is snake oil.
	Here, swallow this pill.
1985 A.D.	That pill is ineffective.
	Here, take this antibiotic.
2000 A.D.	That antibiotic doesn't work anymore.
	Here, eat this root.

Chuckles

After Quasimodo's death, the bishop of the Cathedral of Notre Dame sent word though the streets of Paris that a new bellringer was needed.

The bishop decided that he would conduct the interviews personally and went up into the belfry to begin the screening process. After observing several applicants demonstrate their skills, he decided to call it a day when a lone, armless man approached him and announced that he was there to apply for the bellringer's job.

The bishop was incredulous. "You have no arms!" "No matter" said the man "Observe!" He then began striking the bells with his face, producing a beautiful melody on the carillon.

The bishop listened in astonishment, convinced that he had finally found a suitable replacement for Quasimodo.

Suddenly, rushing forward to strike a bell, the armless man tripped and plunged headlong out of the belfry window to his death in the street below.

The stunned bishop rushed to his side. When he reached the street a crowd had gathered around the fallen figure drawn by the beautiful music they had heard only moments before.

As they silently parted to let the bishop through, one of them asked "Bishop" who was this man?"

"I don't know his name," the bishop sadly replied "but his face rings a bell." *(but wait, there's more to the story)*

The following day, despite the sadness that weighed heavily on his heart due to the unfortunate death of the armless bellringer, the bishop continued his interviews for a new bellringer of Notre Dame.

The first man to approach him said "Your Excellency, I am the brother of the poor armless wretch that fell to his death from this very belfry yesterday. I pray that you honour his life by allowing me to replace him in this duty."

The bishop agreed to give the man an audition and as the armless man's brother stooped to pick up a mallet to strike the first bell, he groaned, clutched at his chest and died on the spot.

Two monks, hearing the bishop's cries of grief at this second tragedy, rushed up the stairs to his side. "What has happened?" the first breathlessly asked, "Who is this man?"

"I don't know his name," sighed the distraught bishop, "but he's a dead ringer for his brother."

☺ When weeding, the best way to make sure you are removing a weed and not a valuable plant is to pull on it. If it comes out of the ground easily, it is a valuable plant.

☺ One good turn gets most of the blankets.

☺ There are two kinds of pedestrians: the quick and the dead!

☺ It's not hard to meet expenses, they are everywhere.

☺ Before marriage, a man yearns for the woman he loves. After marriage the "Y" becomes silent.

ACTUAL LABEL INSTRUCTIONS ON CONSUMER GOODS

ON SEARS HAIR DRYER: Do not use while sleeping.

BAG OF FRITOS: You could be a winner!
No purchase necessary. Details inside.

SOME SWANN FROZEN DINNERS: Serving suggestion. Defrost.

ON MARKS & SPENCER'S BREAD PUDDING:
Product will be hot after heating.

ON NYTOL (a sleep aid): May cause drowsiness.

ON A KOREAN KITCHEN KNIFE: Warning: keep out of children.

In the Bronx, N.Y. lived a rich cat who was a bit of a snob, though she did deign to chat on occasion with her neighbour, an alley cat. One day she announced that she was going to have an operation but she didn't say what for. Two weeks later her humble friend saw her again and inquired politely how she was feeling, then dared to ask what kind of an operation she had had.

"Oh, I am quite well now, thank you," the rich cat replied, stiffly. "I had a hysterectomy."

"For heaven's sake!" the alley cat exclaimed in exasperation... "Why can't you call a spayed a spayed???"

☻ Seems that a tribal chieftain's daughter was offered as a bride to the son of a neighboring potentate in exchange for two cows and four sheep.

The big swap was to be effected on the shore of the stream that separated the two tribes.

Pop and his daughter showed up at the appointed time only to discover that the groom and his livestock were on the other side of the stream.

The father grunted..."The fool doesn't know which side his bride is bartered on."

☻ A man was walking along a California beach and stumbled across an old lamp. He picked it up and rubbed it and out popped a genie.

The genie said "OK, OK, You released me from the lamp, blah, blah, blah. This is the fourth time this month and I'm getting a little sick of these wishes so you can forget about three. You only get one wish."

The man sat and thought about it for a while and said, "I've always wanted to go to Hawaii but I'm scared to fly and I get seasick on a boat. Could you build me a bridge to Hawaii so I can drive over there to visit?"

The genie laughed and said 'That's impossible. Think of the logistics of that! How would the supports ever reach the bottom of the Pacific? Think of how much concrete...how much steel! No, think of another wish." The man said OK and tried to think of a really good wish.

Finally, he said "I've been married and divorced four times. My wives always said that I don't care and that I'm insensitive. So I wish that I could understand women...know how they feel inside and what they are thinking when they give me the silent treatment...know why they're crying, know what they really want when they say "nothing"...know how to make them truly happy..."

The genie said, "You want that bridge two lanes or four?"

A woman got on a bus holding a baby. The bus driver said. "That's the ugliest baby I've EVER seen!"

In a huff, the woman slammed her fare into the fare box and took an aisle seat near the rear of the bus. She fumed for a few stops and started getting really worked up. The man seated next to her sensed that she was agitated and asked her what was wrong.

"The bus driver insulted me!" she fumed. The man sympathized and said, "Hey! He's a public servant and he shouldn't say things to insult the passengers."

"You're right!" she said. "I think I'll go back up there and give him a piece of my mind."

"That's a good idea," the man said. "Here, let me hold your monkey!"

The French are known for their love of unusual gourmet foods, so a young cook decided that the French would enjoy feasting on rabbits. He decided to raise rabbits in Paris and sell them to the finer restaurants in the city. He searched all over Paris seeking a suitable place to raise his rabbits. None could be found. Finally, an old priest at the cathedral said he could have a small area behind the rectory for his rabbits. He successfully raised a number of them and when he went about Paris selling them, a restaurant owner asked him where he got such fresh rabbits.

The young man replied "I raise them myself, near the cathedral. In fact, I have...A HUTCH BACK OF NOTRE DAME.

ACTUAL CLASSIFIED ADS

Amana Washer $100 -
Owned by clean bachelor
who seldom washed.

Snow Blower for Sale -
Only used on snowy days.

Free Puppies - Part German Shepherd - part dog.

2 Wire Mesh Butchering Gloves: 1 5-finger, 1 3-finger,
Pair $15.

Tickle Me Elmo, Still in Box, Comes with its own 1988
mustang, 56L Auto, Excellent condition $6,800.

Cows, Calves Never Bred. Also 1 Gay Bull for Sale.

83 Toyota Hunchback - $2,000.

Bar S Sliced Bologna - Regular or Tasty.
Save 30 cents on 2.

For Sale: Lee Majors (6 Million Dollar Man) $50.

Shakespeare's Pizza - Free Chopsticks.

 *Chuckles*

Q. What did the fish say when it hit a concrete wall?
A. Dam!!!

Q. What do eskimos get from sitting on the ice too long?
A. Polaroids

Q. What do you call Santa's helpers?
A. Subordinate clauses.

Q. What's the difference between roast beef and pea soup?
A. Anyone can roast beef.

Q. What lies at the bottom of the ocean and twitches?
A. A nervous wreck.

Q. Where do you find a dog with no legs?
A. Exactly where you left him.

Q. Why do gorillas have big nostrils?
A. Because they have big fingers.

Q. What do you call cheese that doesn't belong to you?
A. Nacho cheese.

Q. Why don't blind people like to sky dive?
A. Because it scares the hell out of the dog.

One day, a large group of people were waiting for the bus at a local Greyhound station. At the front of the line was a very attractive woman dressed in a black business vest, white blouse, leather miniskirt and high heels.

As the bus pulled up and opened the door, she went to board it but found that her skirt was too tight for her to raise her leg to the required height. Looking around and thinking quickly, she reached behind her and undid the zipper on the back of her skirt a little and then tried again.

Again, she found that she could not manage the step so once more she reached behind her and unzipped her skirt a little more. With a smile she looked at the bus driver and tried to board again. Still she found that she could not step that high and so with exasperation and a sigh she unzipped her skirt the rest of the way down. To her amazement, her leg still would not reach the bottom step.

Finally, a very large Texan behind her gently grabbed her by the waist, lifted her up and placed her on the bus.

The woman tuned to the Texan furious and said "Who do you think you are to touch my body in that way? I don't even know you!"

The Texan looked at her and replied, "Well Ma'am, after you unzipped my fly I thought we were pretty good friends."

(More) Fractured Medical Terms

Benign ....*What you be after you is eight.*

Artery ....*The study of paintings.*

Bacteria ....*Back door to the cafeteria.*

Cesarean Section ....*A neighbourhood in Rome.*

Catscan ....*Searching for kitty.*

Colic ....*A sheep dog.*

Coma ....*A punctuation mark.*

Fester ....*Quicker than someone else.*

G.I. Series ....*World series of military baseball.*

Hangnail ....*Something to hang your coat on.*

Impotent ....*Distinguished, well known.*

Labor Pain ....*Getting hurt at work.*

Medical Staff ....*A doctor's cane.*

Morbid ....*A higher offer.*

Nitrates ....*Cheaper than day rates.*

Outpatient ....*A person who has fainted.*

Pelvis ....*Paternal cousin to Elvis.*

Post Operative ....*A letter carrier.*

Recovery Room ....*Place to do upholstery.*

Secretion ....*Hiding something.*

Tablet ....*A small table.*

Terminal illness ....*Getting sick at the airport.*

Tumor ....*One plus one more.*

Varicose ....*Nearby.*

A big-city California lawyer went duck hunting in rural Texas. He shot and dropped a bird, but it fell into a farmer's field on the other side of a fence. As the lawyer climbed over the fence, an elderly farmer drove up on his tractor and asked him what he was doing.

The litigator responded, "I shot a duck and it fell in this field, and now I'm going to retrieve it." The old farmer replied, "This is my property and you are not coming over here."

The indignant lawyer said, "I am one of the best trial attorneys in the U.S. and, if you don't let me get that duck, I'll sue you and take everything you own." The old farmer smiled and said, "Apparently, you don't know how we do things in Texas. We settle small disagreements like this with the Texas Three-Kick Rule." The lawyer asked, "What is the Texas Three-Kick Rule?"

The farmer replied, "Well, first I kick you three times and then you kick me three times, and so on, back and forth, until someone gives up." The attorney quickly thought about the proposed contest and decided that he could easily take the old codger. He agreed to abide by local custom.

The old farmer slowly climbed down from the tractor and walked up to the city feller. His first kick planted the toe of his heavy work boot into the lawyer's groin and dropped him to his knees. His second kick nearly wiped the man's nose off his face. The barrister was flat on his belly when the farmer's third kick to a kidney nearly caused him to give up.

The lawyer summoned every bit of his will, managed to get to his feet and said, "Okay you old coot - now it's my turn."

The old farmer grinned and said, "Naww, I give up; you can have the duck."

 *Chuckles*

THINGS NOT TO SAY TO A POLICEMAN

I can't reach my license unless you hold my beer.

Sorry, Officer, I didn't realize my radar detector wasn't plugged in.

You're not going to check the trunk, are you?

Gee Officer, that's terrific! The last officer only gave me a warning, too.

Do you know why you pulled me over? Okay, just so one of us does.

I was trying to keep up with traffic. Yes, I know there are no other cars around...that's how far ahead of me they are.

If the Officer says "Your eyes look red, have you been drinking?", don't respond with, "Your eyes look glazed, have you been eating doughnuts?"

Sigmund Freud actually died one day. After taking a bath, he fell getting out of the tub and fractured his skull, killing him instantly......... might this be called a Freudian slip???

WOMEN'S BUMPER STICKERS

SO MANY MEN, SO FEW WHO CAN AFFORD ME

IF THEY DON'T HAVE CHOCOLATE IN HEAVEN, I AIN'T GOING.

MY MOTHER IS A TRAVEL AGENT FOR GUILT TRIPS

PRINCESS, HAVING HAD SUFFICIENT EXPERIENCE WITH PRINCES, SEEKS FROG

COFFEE, CHOCOLATE, MEN...SOME THINGS ARE JUST BETTER RICH

IF YOU WANT BREAKFAST IN BED, SLEEP IN THE KITCHEN

DINNER IS READY WHEN THE SMOKE ALARM GOES OFF

WARNING: I HAVE AN ATTITUDE AND I KNOW HOW TO USE IT.

OF COURSE I DON'T LOOK BUSY...I DID IT RIGHT THE FIRST TIME.

YOU HAVE THE RIGHT TO REMAIN SILENT, SO PLEASE....

A Letter To The Bank

This is an actual letter sent to a bank in the U.S. The bank thought it amusing enough to publish in the New York Times.

Dear Sir:

I am writing to thank you for bouncing the check with which I endeavored to pay my plumber last month. By my calculations some three nanoseconds must have elapsed between his presenting the check and the arrival in my account of the funds needed to honor it. I refer, of course, to the automatic monthly deposit of my entire salary, an arrangement which, I admit, has only been in place for eight years. You are to be commended for seizing that brief window of opportunity and also for debiting my account with $50 by way of penalty for the inconvenience I caused your bank.

My thankfulness springs from the manner in which this incident has caused me to rethink my errant financial ways. You have set me on the path of fiscal righteousness. No more will our relationship be blighted by these unpleasant incidents, for I am restructuring my affairs in 2000, taking as my model the procedures, attitudes and conduct of your very bank. I can think of no greater compliment, and I know you will be excited and proud to hear it.

To this end, please be advised about the following changes. I have noticed that whereas I personally attend to your telephone calls and letters, when I try to contact you, I am confronted by the impersonal, every-changing, prerecorded, faceless entity, which your bank has become. From now on I, like you, choose only to deal with a flesh and blood person. My mortgage and loan repayments will, therefore and hereafter, no longer be automatic, but will arrive at your bank, by check, addressed personally and confidentially to an employee of your branch, whom you must nominate. You will be aware that it is an offense under the Postal Act for any other person to open such an envelope.

Please find attached an Application for Authorized Contact Status which I require your chosen employee to complete. I am sorry it runs to eight pages, but in order that I know as much about him or her as your bank knows about me, there is no alternative. Please note that all copies of his or her medical history must be countersigned by a Justice of the Peace, and that the mandatory details of his/her financial situation (income, debts, assets and liabilities) must be accompanied by documented proof. In due course I will issue your employee with a PIN number which he/she must quote in all dealings with me. I regret that it cannot be shorter than 28 digits but, again, I have modeled it on the number of button presses required to access my account balance on your phone bank service. As they say, imitation is the sincerest form of flattery.

Let me level the playing field even further by introducing you to my new telephone system, which you will notice, is very much like yours. My Authorized Contact at your bank, the only person with whom I will have any dealings, may call me at any time and will be answered by an automated voice. Press buttons as follows:

1) To make an appointment to see me
2) To query a missing payment
3) To transfer the call to my living room in case I am there
4) To transfer the call to my bedroom in case I am sleeping
5) To transfer the call to my toilet in case I am attending to nature
6) To transfer the call to my mobile phone in case I am not at home
7) To leave a message on my computer (to leave a message a password to access my computer is required; password will be communicated at a later date to the Authorized Contact.)
8) To return to the main menu and listen carefully to options 1 through 7.
9) To make a general complaint or inquiry, the Authorized Contact will then be put on hold, pending the attention of my automated answering service. While this may, on occasion, involve a lengthy wait, uplifting music will play for the duration. This month I've chose a refrain from "The Best of Woody Guthrie":

"Oh the banks are made of marble, with a guard at every door,
And the vaults are filled with silver, that the miners sweated for." ...
...after twenty minutes of that, our mutual contact will know it by heart.

On a more serious note, we come to the matter of cost. As your bank has often pointed out, the ongoing drive for greater efficiency comes at a cost, a cost which you have always been quick to pass on to me. Let me repay your kindness by passing some costs back.

First, there is the matter of advertising material you send me. This I will read for a fee of $20 per page.

Inquiries from your Authorized Contact will be billed at $5 per minute of my times spent in response. Any debits to my account, as, for example, in the matter of the penalty for the dishonored check, will be passed back to you.

My new phone service runs at 75 cents a minute (even Woody Guthrie doesn't come for free), so you would be well advised to keep your inquiries brief and to the point.

Regrettably, but again following your example, I must also levy an establishment fee of 2% of my balance or $50 (whichever is more) to cover the setting up of this new arrangement.

May I wish you a happy, if ever-so-slightly less prosperous, New Year.

Your humble client.

REPLIES THAT HAD TEACHERS CHUCKLING WHILE CORRECTING ELEMENTARY SCHOOL TEST PAPERS.

✗ "Dinosaurs became extinct after the flood because they were too big to get in the ark."

✗ "Queen Elizabeth was a fat woman. She stoutly resisted the demands of the Spanish ambassador."

✗ "Most of the houses in France are made of plaster of Paris."

✗ "We do not raise silk worms in the U.S. because we get our silk from rayon. He is a larger animal and gives more milk."

✗ "Animal husbandry means having more than one husband."

✗ "Napoleon wanted an heir to the throne but since Josephine was a Baroness, she could not bear children."

✗ "The four seasons are salt, pepper, mustard and vinegar."

✗ "The word trousers is an uncommon noun because it is singular at the top and plural at the bottom."

✗ "Blood circulates in the body by flowing down one leg and up the other."

✗ "Iron was discovered because someone smelt it."

✗ "Strategy is when you don't let the enemy know you are out of ammunition but keep on firing."

✗ "A city purifies its water supply by filtering the water and then forcing it through an aviator."

✗ "The spinal column is a long bunch of bones. The head sits on the top and you sit on the bottom."

✗ "One of the main causes of dust is janitors."

✗ "A scout obeys all to whom obedience is due and respects all duly constipated authorities."

✗ "One by-product of cattle raising is calves."

✗ "New Zealand is a democratic country. They passed a law there preventing women from sweating in the factories."

✗ "Oliver Cromwell had a large, red nose, but under it were deeply religious feelings."

✗ "Manhattan Island was bought from the Indians for $24 and I do not suppose you could buy it now for $500."

✗ "The Civil War was caused by Lincoln signing the Emasculation Proclamation."

✗ "In the spring salmon swim upstream to spoon."

✗ "The difference between a president and a king is that a king has no vice."

Once upon a time a beautiful, independent, self-assured princess happened upon a frog in a pond. The frog said to the princess, "I was once a handsome prince until an evil witch put a spell on me. One kiss from you and I will turn back into a prince and then we can marry, move into the castle with my mom, and you can prepare my meals, clean my clothes, bear my children and forever feel happy doing so."

That night, while the the princess dined on frog legs, she smiled as she said .... "In your dreams, froggy."

Chuckles

A newly established lawyer, wanting to impress the first client coming into his office, picked up the phone and said, "I'm sorry, but I have a tremendous case load and won't be able to look into this for at least a month." He then hung up, turned to the young man in his office and asked "What can I do for you, sir?"

"Nothing" replied the young man, "I'm just here to hook up your phone."

A Texan visiting Newfoundland, stopped in at a farm and sat on the front porch with the farmer. The Texan remarked at the size of the land and the farmer replied, "Yup, and it's all mine. The whole 2 acres." The Texan turned and said, "Well buddy, in Texas, you can get in your car and drive all day and never get off your land."

The farmer sat a while chewing on the end of a piece of straw and finally said, "Yup, I used to have a car like that."

Two vultures boarded an airplane, each carrying two dead raccoons. The stewardess looked at them and said:

"I'm sorry, gentlemen, only one carrion allowed per passenger."

A group of friars were behind in their belfry payments so they opened up a small florist shop to raise funds. Since everyone liked to buy flowers from the men of God, a rival florist across town thought the competition was unfair. He asked the good fathers to close down, but they would not. He went back and begged the friars to close. They ignored him. So, the rival florist hired Hugh MacTaggart, the roughest and most vicious thug in town to "persuade" them to close. Hugh beat up the friars and trashed their store, saying he'd be back if they didn't close up shop.

Terrified, they did so, thereby proving that...
(are you ready?, you're sure??? O.K. here it is)
... Hugh, and only Hugh, can prevent florist friars....

😊 A rope walks into a bar and sits down. The bartender walks over and tells it, "Sorry. We don't serve ropes in here." The rope walks outside and asks a passerby, "Will you do me a favour please? Tie me up and unravel me a little bit. Then scrape me along the sidewalk a little bit." The passerby complies and the rope is definitely looking the worse for wear.

The rope walks back into the bar and sits down. The bartender walks over and asks. "Aren't you the rope that was in her a few minutes ago wanting to be served and I told you we don't serve ropes in here?"

"Nope, I'm a frayed knot." came the reply.

A man goes to his vet and asks "Got anything to cure fleas on a dog?" The vet replies, "That depends. What's wrong with them?"

😊 A Sunday School teacher asked her little children as they were on the way to church service, "And why is it necessary to be quiet in church?"

One bright little girl replied, "Because people are sleeping."

😊 In the same Sunday School the class was studying the Ten Commandments. They were ready to discuss the last one. The teacher asked if anyone could tell her what it was. Susie raised her hand, stood tall, and quoted, "Thou shall not take the covers off thy neighbour's wife."

😊 Miss Jones had been giving her second graders a lesson on science. She had explained about magnets and showed how they would pick up nails and other bits of iron. Now it was question time and she asked: "My name begins with the letter M and I pick up things. What am I?"

A little boy in the front row said: "You're a mother."

Chuckles

***If Wal-Mart is lowering prices every day,
how come nothing is free yet ? ? ? ? ?***

Two buddies Bob and Earl were two of the biggest baseball fans in America. Their entire lives they discussed baseball history in the winter and they pored over every box score during the season. They went to 60 games a year. They even agreed that whoever died first would try to come back and tell the other if there was baseball in heaven.

One summer night, Bob passed away in his sleep after watching the Yankee victory earlier in the evening. He died happy.

A few nights later, his buddy Earl awoke to the sound of Bob's voice from beyond.

"Bob, is that you?" Earl asked.

"Of course its me," Bob replied.

"This is unbelievable!" Earl exclaimed. "So tell me, is there baseball in heaven?"

"Well, I have some good news and some bad news for you. Which do you want to hear first?"

"Tell me the good news first."

"Well, the good news is that yes, there is baseball in heaven, Earl."

"Oh, that's wonderful! So what could possibly be the bad news?"

"You're pitching tomorrow night."

***VENI, VIDI, VISA:
I came,
I saw,
I went shopping.***

☻ A young boy was in a relative's wedding. As he was coming down the aisle he would take two steps, stop, and turn to the crowd. While facing the crowd he would put his hands up like claws and roar. So it went, step by step, ROAR, step, step, ROAR, all the way down the aisle. As you can imagine, the crowd was near tears from laughing so hard by the time he reached the pulpit. The little boy, however, was getting more and more distressed from all the laughing, and was also near tears by the time he reached the pulpit.

When asked what he was doing, the child sniffed and said, "I was being the Ring Bear."

☻ How long a minute is depends on what side of the bathroom door you're on.

☻ Two priests were talking together and the older one said to the younger, "You know, when you came into church with all your new ideas, I had questions about how you were going to fit in and how well your ideas were going to work."

"When you wanted to put bucket seats down in the front two rows of seats, I had my doubts. But now, at every mass, the seats are filled up with young people, so I have to agree that it was a good idea."

"Then, when you wanted to jazz up the choir and we started singing newer, peppier songs, I was afraid it would offend the parishioners. Now we have a lot of new, younger choir members, and the music seems to pick up the services a lot more than the old music. So, once again I have to agree that you were right!"

"When you wanted to put in the drive-through confessional, I have to admit I thought you'd lost it. But now, at least, since there are more people coming to confession than ever, I think you've come up with another good idea.....however, ...the neon sign out front that says 'Toot 'n tell or go to hell' has got to go!"

☻ Did you hear that NASA recently put a bunch of Holsteins into low earth orbit?

They called it the herd shot 'round the world.'

A man is sitting in an airliner which is about to takeoff when another man with a Labrador Retriever occupies the empty seat alongside. The Labrador is situated in the middle, and the first man is looking quizzically at the dog when the second man explains that he and the dog work for the airline.

The airline rep said, "Don't mind Sniffer; he is a sniffing dog, the best there is; I'll show you once we get airborne when I put him to work."

The plane takes off and levels out and the handler says to the first man, "Watch this." He tells the dog, "Sniffer, search."

Sniffer jumps down, walks along the aisle and sits next to a woman for a few seconds. It then returns to its seat and puts one paw on the handler's arm. He says "Good boy."

The airline rep turns to the first man and says, "That woman is in possession of marijuana, so I'm making a note of this and her seat number for the police who will apprehend her on arrival." "Fantastic!" replies the first man.

Once again the rep sends Sniffer to search the aisles. The Lab sniffs about, sits down beside a man for a few seconds, returns to its seat, and places two paws on the handler's arm. The airline rep says "That man is carrying cocaine, so again I'm making a note of this and the seat number." "I like it," says the first man.

A third time the rep sends Sniffer to search the aisles. Sniffer goes up and down the plane and after a while sits down next to someone.

He then comes racing back down the aisle, shaking uncontrollably; jumps up onto his seat and messes all over the place.

The first man is completely disgusted by this behavior from a supposedly well trained sniffing dog and asks, "What the devil is going on here?"

The handler nervously replies, "He just found a bomb!"

Daffy-nitions!

Abdicate
- to give up all hope of ever having a flat stomach.

Carcinoma
- a valley in California, notable for its heavy smog.

Esplanade
- to attempt an explanation while drunk.

Flabbergasted
- appalled at the amount of weight you have gained.

Lymph
- to talk with a lisp

Circumvent
- the opening in the front of boxer shorts.

Balderdash
- a rapidly receding hairline.

Coffee
- a person who is coughed upon.

 *Chuckles*

THINGS THAT MAKE YOU GO HMMM??

If Fed Ex and UPS were to merge, would they call it Fed UP?

If quitters never win, and winners never quit, what fool came up with "Quit while you're ahead"?

Do Lipton employees take coffee breaks?

What hair color do they put on the driver's license of a bald man?

Should they put pictures of missing husbands on beer cans?

Do people read the Bible a whole lot more as they get older because they are cramming for their finals?

*Since mothers feed their babies with little tiny spoons,
- do Chinese mothers use toothpicks?*

Why do they put pictures of criminals up in the Post Office? Are we supposed to write to these men? Why don't they just put their pictures on the postage stamps so the mailmen can look for them while they deliver the mail?

How much deeper would oceans be if sponges didn't live there?

Would a fly without wings be called a "walk"?

Why did kamikaze pilots wear helmets?

Is it true that cannibals don't eat clowns because they taste funny?

T-SHIRT SLOGANS

"Frankly, Scallop, I don't give a clam."

*Wrinkled was not one of the things
I wanted to be when I grew up.*

*Ham & Eggs: A day's work for a chicken,
a lifetime commitment for a pig.*

My dog can lick anyone.

FROM THE MOUTHS OF BABES

"Never trust a dog to watch your
food." *Jonathan, Age 10*

"Never pee on an electric fence."
Chris, Age 13

"Never hold a cat and a
dustbuster at the same time."
Cindy, Age 9

"When your mom is mad at your dad, don't let her brush
your hair." *Sophie, Age 11*

"When you get a bad grade in school, show it to your mom
when she's on the phone." *Kelly, Age 13*

"Felt markers are no good to use as lipstick." *Laurie, Age 9*

Chuckles

The teacher gave her fifth grade class an assignment...Get their parents to tell them a story with a moral at the end of it. The next day the kids came back and one by one began to tell their stories.

Ashley said "My father's a farmer and we have a lot of egg-laying hens. One time we were taking our eggs to market in a basket on the front seat of the pickup truck when we hit a big bump in the road and all the eggs went flying and broke and made a mess."

"And what's the moral of the story?" the teacher asked.

"Don't put all your eggs in one basket!" Ashley replied.

'Very good" said the teacher.

Next, little Sarah raised her hand and said "Our family are farmers too. But we raise chickens for the market. We had a dozen eggs one time, but when they hatched we only got ten live chicks, and the moral to this story is don't count your chickens before they're hatched."

"That was a fine story, Sarah," said the teacher. Michael do you have a story to share?"

"Yes, ma'am. My daddy told me this story about my Aunt Karen. Aunt Karen was a flight engineer in Desert Storm and her plane got hit. She had to bail out over enemy territory and all she had was a bottle of whiskey, a machine gun and a machete. She drank the whiskey on the way down so it wouldn't break and then she landed right in the middle of one hundred enemy troops. She killed seventy of them with the machine gun until she ran out of bullets. Then she killed twenty more with the machete until the blade broke. And then she killed the last ten with her bare hands."

"Good heavens" said the teacher, "what kind of moral did your Daddy tell you from that horrible story?"

"Stay away from Aunt Karen when she's been drinking," replied little Michael.

 # BUMPER STICKERS

FAILURE IS NOT AN OPTION.
IT COMES BUNDLED WITH THE SOFTWARE

A HANGOVER IS THE WRATH OF GRAPES

MY HUSBAND AND I DIVORCED OVER RELIGIOUS
REASONS. HE THOUGHT HE WAS GOD AND I DIDN'T.

I HAVE A DEGREE IN LIBERAL ARTS -
DO YOU WANT FRIES WITH THAT?

PROCRASTINATE NOW!

IF YOU DRINK, DON'T DRIVE, DON'T EVEN PUTT.

SAVE THE WHALES, COLLECT THE WHOLE SET.

DRIVE DEFENSIVELY, BUY A TANK.

IT'S LONELY AT THE TOP BUT YOU EAT BETTER.

VERY FUNNY, SCOTTY.
NOW BEAM DOWN MY CLOTHES!

Chuckles

The local veterinarian in a small town in Maine is known for his wry sense of humour. One summer day a city dog was brought to him after an encounter with a porcupine. After almost an hour of prying, pulling, cutting and stitching, he returned the dog to it's owner who asked what she owed. "Thirty dollars, Ma'am" he answered.

"Why that's simply outrageous!" she stormed. "That's what's wrong with you Maine people, you're always trying to overcharge summer visitors. Whatever do you do in the winter, when we're not around to overcharge?"

"Raise porcupines, ma'am" answered the doctor.

Have you heard about the cat who ate the cheese and sat by the mousehole with baited breath?

Barbara Walters had done a story on gender roles in Kuwait several years before the Gulf War and she noted then that women customarily walked 10 feet behind their husbands.

She returned to Kuwait recently and observed that the men now walked several yards behind their wives. Ms. Walters approached one of the women for an explanation.

"This is marvelous" she said. "What enabled women here to achieve this reversal of roles?" The Kuwaiti woman replied "Land mines".

The newlyweds went on a cruise for their honeymoon and found themselves shipwrecked on an island where a tribe of cannibals lived. Nevertheless, the inhabitants were very welcoming. In fact, when they found out the couple had just been married, the cannibals threw a party.

They toasted the bride, then barbequed the groom.

MY WILD OATS HAVE TURNED TO SHREDDED WHEAT.

Chuckles

"A cajun named Jean Paul, moved to Texas and bought a donkey from an old farmer for $100. The farmer agreed to deliver the donkey the next day.

The next day, the farmer drove up and said, "Sorry, but I have some bad news. The donkey died."

"Well, then, just give me my money back."

"Can't do that, I went and spent it already."

"O.K. then, just unload the donkey."

"What ya gonna do with him?"

"I'm going to raffle him off."

"You can't raffle off a dead donkey!"

"Sure I can. Watch me. I just won't tell anybody he's dead."

A month later the farmer met up with the Cajun and asked, "What happened with that dead donkey?"

"I raffled him off. I sold 500 tickets at two dollars apiece and made a profit of $898."

"Didn't anyone complain?"

"Just the guy who won. So I gave him his two dollars back."

A mechanic was removing a cylinder head from the motor of a Harley when he spotted a world famous heart surgeon in his shop.

The heart surgeon was waiting for the service manager to come take a look at his bike. The mechanic shouted across the garage, "Hey Doc, can I ask you a question?"

The surgeon, a bit surprised, walked over to the mechanic working on the motorcycle.

The mechanic straightened up, wiped his hands on a rag and asked, "So Doc, look at this engine. I also can open it up, take valves out, fix 'em, put in new parts and when I finish this, it'll work just like a new one. So how come I get a pittance and you get the really big money when you and I are doing basically the same work?"

The surgeon paused, smiled and leaned over and whispered to the mechanic... "Try doing it while it's running!"

All You Need To Know About Life You Can Learn From The Easter Bunny

Don't put all your eggs in one basket.

Walk softly and carry a big carrot.

Everyone needs a friend who is all ears.

There's no such thing as too much candy.

All work and no play can make you a basket case.

Everyone is entitled to a bad hare day.

Let happy thoughts multiply like rabbits.

Some body parts should be floppy.

Keep your paws off other people's jellybeans.

Good things come in small sugar-coated packages.

The grass is always greener in someone else's basket.

The best things in life are still sweet and gooey!

Chuckles

Why We Love Children

A kindergarten pupil told his teacher he'd found a cat in his backyard. She asked him if it was dead or alive. "Dead" she was informed.

"How do you know?" she asked her pupil. "Because I pissed in its ear and it didn't move" answered the child innocently.

"You did WHAT?" the teacher exclaimed in surprise.

"You know," explained the boy, "I leaned over and went 'Psst' and it didn't move.

An exasperated mother, whose son was always getting into mischief, finally asked him, "How do you expect to get into Heaven?"

The boy thought it over and said "Well, I'll run in and out and keep slamming the door until St. Peter says 'For Heaven's sake, Dylan, come in or stay out!' "

A little boy was doing his math homework. He said to himself, "Two plus five, that son of a bitch is seven. Three plus six, that son of a bitch is nine..." His mother heard what he was saying and gasped. "What are you doing?" The little boy answered, "I'm doing my math homework, Mom."

"And this is how you teacher taught you to do it?" the mother asked.

"Yes," he answered.

Infuriated, the mother asked the teacher the next day "What are you teaching my son in math?" The teacher replied "Right now, we are learning addition."

The mother asked, "And are you teaching them to say two plus two that son of a bitch is four?"

After the teacher stopped laughing, she answered, "What I taught them was, two plus two, THE SUM OF WHICH is four."

A small boy is sent to bed by his father.
Five minutes later..."Da-ad.."
"What?"
"I'm thirsty. Can you bring me a drink of water?"
"No. You had your chance. Lights out."
Five minutes later: "Da-aaad..."
"WHAT?"
"I'm THIRSTY. Can I please have a drink of water??"
"I told you NO! If you ask again, I'll have to spank you!"
Five minutes later...."Da-aaad..."
"WHAT?"
"When you come in to spank me, can you bring a drink of water?"

A man wins a free ticket to the SuperBowl from his company. Unfortunately, when he arrives at the stadium he is closer to the Goodyear Blimp than the field. About half way through the first quarter he notices an empty seat ten rows off the field right on the 50 yard line.

He decides to take a chance and makes his way through the stadium around the security guards to the empty seat.

As he sits down, he asked the gentleman sitting next to him, "Excuse me, is anyone sitting here?" The man replies "No".

Now, very excited to be in such a great seat for the game, he again inquires of the man next to him, "This is incredible! Who, in their right mind, would have a seat like this at the SuperBowl and not use it?"

The man replies "Well actually, the seat belongs to me. I was supposed to come with my wife, but she passed away. This is the first SuperBowl we haven't been to together since we got married in 1967".

"Well, that's terribly sad. But still, couldn't you find someone to take the seat? A close friend, or a relative?

"No" the man replied. "They're all at the funeral."

Thought for the Day

Never be afraid to try something new. Remember,
amateurs built the ark; professionals built the Titanic.

Love is grand; divorce is a hundred grand.

I am in shape. Round is a shape.

If a kleptomaniac has a cold, does he take something for it?

Time might be a great healer but it's also a lousy beautician.

Brain cells come and brain cells go, but fat cells live forever.

Age doesn't always bring wisdom. Sometimes age comes alone.

Age is a very high price to pay for maturity.

Going to church doesn't make you a Christian anymore than
going to a garage makes you a mechanic.

A closed mouth gathers no feet.

If you must choose between two evils,
pick the one you've never tried before.

It is easier to get forgiveness than permission.

For every action there is an equal and opposite government
program.

Bills travel through the mail at twice the speed of checks.

A conscience is what hurts when all the other parts feel so good.

If you look like your passport picture you probably need the trip.

Life is like a roll of toilet paper. The closer you get to the end, the
faster it goes.

Get Ready to Moan!

A mushroom walks into a bar, sits down and orders a drink. The bartender says, "We don't serve mushrooms in here." The mushroom says, "Why not? I'm a fun guy!"

Why do cows wear bells? Because their horns don't work.

There was a man who entered a pun contest in the local paper. He sent in ten different puns in the hope that at least one would win. Unfortunately, no pun in ten did!

Pearls of Dog Wisdom

- Some days you're the dog; some days you're the hydrant!
- Whoever said you can't buy happiness forgot about puppies.
- A dog teaches a boy fidelity, perseverance and to turn around three times before lying down.
- There is no psychiatrist in the world like a puppy licking your face.

Why Beer Makes You Smarter!

A herd of buffalo can only move as fast as the slowest buffalo. When the herd is hunted, it is the slowest and weakest ones at the back of the herd that are killed first. This natural selection is good for the herd as a whole because the general speed and health of the whole group keeps improving by the regular killing of the weakest members.

In much the same way, the human brain can only operate as fast as the slowest brain cells. Excessive intake of alcohol kills brain cells, but naturally it attacks the slowest and weakest brain cells first.

In this way, regular consumption of beer eliminates weaker brain cells, making the brain a faster and more efficient machine. That's why you always feel smarter after a few beers.

ONLY IN AMERICA...

• do drugstores make the sick walk all the way to the back of the store to get their prescription while healthy people can buy cigarettes at the front.

• do we have drive-up ATM machines with braille lettering.

• can a pizza get to your home faster than an ambulance.

• do banks leave both doors open and then chain the pens to the counters.

• do people order double cheeseburgers, large fries and a diet coke.

• do we leave cars worth hundreds of thousands of dollars in the driveway and put our useless junk in the garage.

• do we buy hot dogs in packages of 12 and buns in packages of 8.

• are there handicap parking places in front of a skating rink.

• do we use the word "politics" to describe the process so well. "Poli" in Latin meaning many and "tics" meaning blood sucking creatures.

Great Truths About Life
That Little Children Have Learned

- *No matter how hard you try, you can't baptize a cat.*
- *If your sister hits you, don't hit her back.*
  They always catch the second person.
- *Never ask your 3-year old brother to*
  hold a tomato.
- *School lunches stick to the wall.*
- *You can't hide a piece of broccoli in a*
  glass of milk.
- *Don't wear polka-dot underwear under white shorts.*
- *The best place to be when you're sad*
  is Grandpa's lap.

Great Truths About Life
That Adults Have Learned

- *Raising teenagers is like nailing jello to a tree.*
- *There is always a lot to be thankful for if you take the*
  time to look. For example, I'm sitting here thinking
  how nice it is that wrinkles don't hurt.
- *Car sickness is the feeling you get when the monthly*
  payment is due.
- *Families are like fudge. Mostly sweet, with a few nuts.*
- *Today's mighty oak is just yesterday's oak that held its*
  ground.
- *Middle age is when you choose your cereal for the*
  fiber, not the toy.
- *You know that you're getting old when you stoop to tie*
  your shoe and wonder what else you can do while
  you're down there

The Cowboy's Guide To Life

- Don't squat with yer spurs on.

- Letting the cat outta the bag is a whole lot easier 'n puttin' it back in.

- If yer riding ahead of the herd, take a look behind you every now and then to make sure it's still there.

- After eating an entire bull, a mountain lion felt so good he started roaring. He kept it up until a hunter came along and shot him. The moral: "When yer full of bull, keep yer mouth shut."

- Never kick a cow chip on a hot day.

- There's two theories to arguin' with a woman. Neither one works.

- Never slap a man who's chewin' tobacco.

- Always drink upstream from the herd.

- The quickest way to double yer money is to fold it over and put it back in yer pocket.

- Never miss a good chance to shut up.

- There are three kinds of men. The kind that learns by reading, the few who learn by observation and the rest who have to pee on the electric fence for themselves.

THE PHONE WON'T STOP RINGING!

Sophie Martin of Athens, Tennessee had a serious telephone problem. The brand new $10 million Plaza Hotel opened nearby and had acquired almost the same phone number as Sophie.

From the moment the hotel opened, Sophie was besieged by calls not for her. Since she had the same number for years, she felt that she had a cause to persuade the hotel management to change its number.

The management stoutly refused, claiming it could not change its stationary. The phone company was not helpful either. Just because a customer was getting someone else's calls 24 hours a day didn't make it responsible.

After her pleas fell on deaf ears, Sophie decided to take matters into her own hands. At 9 o'clock the phone rang. Someone from Memphis was calling and asked for a room the following Tuesday. Sophie said, "No problem, how many nights?"

A few hours later Dallas called. A secretary wanted a suite with two bedrooms for a week. Sophie said the Presidential suite on the 10th floor was available for $600 a night. The secretary said that she would take it and asked if the hotel wanted a deposit. "No, that won't be necessary," said Sophie, "We trust you."

The next day was a busy one for Sophie. In the morning she booked an electric appliance manufacturer's convention for Memorial Day weekend, a college prom and a reunion of the 82nd Airborne veterans from World II.

Her biggest challenge came when a mother called to book the ballroom for her daughter's wedding in June. Sophie assured the woman that it would be no problem and asked if she would like the hotel to provide the flowers. Then she offered a no charge valet service as well.

Within a few months the Hotel was a disaster zone. People kept showing up for weddings, bar mitzvahs and parties and were all told there were no such events.

Sophie had her final revenge when she read that the hotel was close to bankruptcy.

Her phone rang shortly thereafter and an executive from another major hotel chain said, "We're prepared to offer you $200,000.00 for the Plaza Hotel."

Sophie replied, "We'll take it, but only if you change the telephone number."

Out of the Mouths of Babes

A mother was preparing pancakes for her sons, Kevin, 5 and Ryan, 3 yrs. of age.

The boys began to argue over who would get the first pancake. Their mother saw the opportunity for a moral lesson.

If Jesus were sitting here he would say, "Let my brother have the first pancake. I can wait."

Kevin turned to his brother and said, "Ryan, you be Jesus."

After the church service a little boy told the pastor, "When I grow up, I'm going to give you some money."

"Well, thank you," the pastor replied, "but why?"

"Because my daddy says you're one of the poorest preachers we've ever had."

A father was reading Bible stories to his young son. He read, "The man named Lot was warned to take his wife and flee out of the city, but his wife looked back and was turned to salt."

His son asked "What happened to the flea?"

The preacher was wired for sound with a lapel mike and as he preached, he moved briskly about the platform, jerking the mike cord as he went. Then he moved to one side, got wound up in the cord and nearly tripped before jerking it again.

After several circles and jerks, a little girl in the third pew leaned towards her mother and whispered, "If he gets loose, will he hurt us?"

A new neighbour asked the little girl next door if she had any brothers and sisters.

"No," she replied. "I'm a lonely child."

Six year old Angie and her four year old brother Joel were sitting together in church. Joel giggled, sang and talked out loud. Finally his big sister had enough. "You're not supposed to talk out loud in church."

"Why? Who's going to stop me?" Joel asked

Angie pointed to the back of the church and said, "See those two men standing by the door? They're hushers."

The kindergarten teacher was showing her class in the U.S. an encyclopedia page picturing several national flags. She pointed to the U.S. flag and asked, "What flag is this?"

A little girl called out, "That's the flag of our country."

"Very good," the teacher said, "and what is the name of our country?"

"Tis of thee" the girl said confidently.

A mother was telling her little girl what her own childhood was like: "We used to skate outside on a pond. I had a swing made from a tire; it hung from a tree in our front yard. We rode our pony. We picked wild raspberries in the woods."

The little girl was wide-eyed, taking this in. At last she said, "I sure wish I'd gotten to know you sooner!"

121

The Gift

Just before Christmas, a kindergarten teacher was receiving gifts from her pupils.

The florist's son handed her a gift. She shook it, held it overhead and said, "I bet I know what it is; some flowers"

"That's right," the little boy replied, "but how did you know?"

"Oh, just a wild guess," the teacher said.

The next pupil was the candy store owner's daughter. The teacher held her gift overhead, shook it and said: "I bet I can guess what this is; a box of candy."

"That's right, but how did you know?" asked the girl.

"Oh, just a wild guess," the teacher said.

The next gift was from the son of a liquor store owner. The teacher held it overhead, but it was leaking. She touched a drop of the leakage with her finger and touched it to her tongue.

"Is it wine?" she asked.

"No," the boy replied, obviously delighted that he was the first student to at least temporarily defy the teacher's apparent insight.

The teacher repeated the process, touching another drop of the leakage to her tongue. "Is it champagne? she asked.

"No!" the clearly delighted boy answered. Once again the teacher tasted the leakage and finally said, "I give up, I just can't guess, what is it?

The little boy enthusiastically replied, "It's a puppy!"

REASONS TO SMILE

Every seven minutes of every day, someone in an
aerobics class pulls a hamstring.

One of life's mysteries is how a 2 pound box of
candy can make a woman gain 5 lbs.

My mind not only wanders,
it sometimes leaves completely

The best way to forget all your troubles is to wear
tight shoes.

The nice part about living in a small town is that when you
don't know what you're doing, someone else does.

The older you get, the tougher it is to lose weight because
by then, your body and your fat are really good friends.

Amazing, you hang something in a closet for a while
and it shrinks two sizes!

A lady was picking through the frozen turkeys at the grocery
store, but couldn't find one big enough for her family. She
asked the stock boy "Do these turkeys get any bigger?"
To which the stock boy replied: "No ma'am, they're dead."

FUNNIEST NEWSPAPER HEADLINES

WAR DIMS HOPE FOR PEACE

LOCAL HIGH SCHOOL
DROPOUTS CUT IN HALF

POLICE BEGIN CAMPAIGN TO
RUN DOWN JAYWALKERS

PROSTITUTES APPEAL TO POPE

PANDA MATING FAILS; VETERINARIAN TAKES OVER

BRITISH LEFT WAFFLES ON FALKLAND ISLANDS

TEACHER STRIKES IDLE KIDS

CLINTON WINS BUDGET; MORE LIES AHEAD

PLANE TOO CLOSE TO GROUND, CRASH PROBE TOLD

MINERS REFUSE TO WORK AFTER DEATH

JUVENILE COURT TO TRY SHOOTING DEFENDANT

INCLUDE YOUR CHILDREN WHEN BAKING COOKIES

SOMETHING WENT WRONG IN JET CRASH

KIDS MAKE NUTRITIONAL SNACKS

Four men were bragging about how smart their dogs are. The first man was an engineer, the second man was an accountant, the third man was a chemist, the fourth was a government worker.

To show off, the engineer called to his dog, "T-Square, do your stuff."

T-Square trotted over to a desk, took out some paper and a pen and promptly drew a circle, a square and a triangle. Everyone agreed that was pretty smart.

The accountant said his dog could do better. He called his dog and said, "Spreadsheet, do your stuff."

Spreadsheet went out into the kitchen and returned with a dozen cookies. He divided them into four equal piles of three cookies each. Everyone agreed that was good but the chemist said his dog could do better.

He called his dog and said, "Measure, do your stuff."

Measure got up, walked over to the fridge, took out a quart of milk, got a 10 ounce glass from the cupboard and poured exactly 8 ounces of milk without spilling a drop.
Everyone agreed that was good.

Then the three men turned to the government worker and said, "What can your dog do?"

The government worker called to his dog and said, "Coffee Break, do your stuff".

Coffee Break jumped to his feet, ate the cookies, drank the milk, went to the bathroom on the paper, made love to the other three dogs - and claimed he injured his back while doing so - filed a grievance report for unsafe working conditions, put in for Workers Compensation and went home for the rest of the day on sick leave.

Old fishermen never die... they just smell that way!

A Story About The Potato Family

(you can shoot us for this one!)

One night, the Potato family, consisting of Mother Potato and her three daughters, sat down to dinner. Midway through the meal, the eldest daughter spoke up.

"Mother Potato, I have an announcement to make. I'm getting married!"

"Married! That's wonderful! Who are you marrying?" asked mother Potato.

"I'm marrying a Russet," replied the daughter.

"Oh, a Russet is a fine tater," said the mother.

Shortly after the middle daughter spoke and said, "I too am getting married!"

"And who are you marrying, middle daughter?" enquired mother Potato.

"I'm marrying an Idaho!" beamed the middle daughter.

"Oh," mother Potato answered, very pleased, "and an Idaho is a fine tater!"

During all the excitement, the youngest daughter exclaimed, "I hope this won't be too shocking, but I, too, am getting married."

"Really?" said mother Potato with sincere excitement. "Who are you marrying?"

"I'm marrying Dan Rather!"

"Dan Rather?" said mother potato, scowling. "But he's just a common tater!"

Good Questions - ? ? ?

Why are they called stairs inside but steps outside?

Why is there a light in the frige, but not in the freezer?

If croutons are stale bread, why do they come in airtight packages?

Why does mineral water that had trickled through mountains for centuries have a "use by" date?

Why do toasters always have a setting that burns the toast to a horrible crisp no-one would eat?

Is French kissing in France just called kissing?

Who was the first person to look at a cow and say, "I think I'll squeeze these dangly things here and drink whatever comes out."?

What do people in China call their good plates?

If the professor on Gilligan's Island could make a radio out of a coconut, why couldn't he fix a hole in the boat?

If people point to their wrist when asking for the time, what do they point to when they ask where the toilet is?

Can you sentence a homeless man to house arrest?

If having a job is so terrific, how come they have to pay you to do it?

If the #2 pencil is the most popular, why is it still #2?

If one synchronized swimmer drowns, do the rest have to drown too?

If all the world is a stage, where is the audience sitting?

Why is it called tourist season if we can't shoot them?

Do infants enjoy infancy as much as adults enjoy adultery?

Darned if I know, do you?

Chuckles

HOW TO SPEAK ABOUT WOMEN
AND BE POLITICALLY CORRECT:

She is not a BABE or a CHICK - she is a BREASTED AMERICAN.

She is not a BLEACHED BLONDE - She is PEROXIDE DEPENDENT.

She is not a BAD COOK - She is MICROWAVE COMPATIBLE

She is not HALF NAKED - She is WARDROBE IMPAIRED

She is not FAT - She is a METABOLIC UNDERACHIEVER.

She does not WEAR TOO MUCH PERFUME -
She commits FRAGRANCE ABUSE.

HOW TO SPEAK ABOUT MEN
AND BE POLITICALLY CORRECT:

He does not have a BEER GUT -
He has developed a LIQUID GRAIN STORAGE FACILITY.

He is not BALD - He is in FOLLICLE REGRESSION

He does not act like a TOTAL ASS -
He develops a case of RECTAL-CRANIAL INVERSION

He is not a SEX MACHINE - He is ROMANTICALLY AUTOMATED

He is not a MALE CHAUVINIST PIG - He has SWINE EMPATHY

He is not afraid of COMMITMENT -
He is MONOGAMOUSLY CHALLENGED

One day a farmer's donkey fell into an abandoned well. The animal cried piteously for hours as the farmer tried to figure out what to do.

Finally, he decided the animal was old and the well needed to be covered anyway, so it just wasn't worth it to him to try to retrieve the donkey.

He invited all his neighbors to come over and help him. They each grabbed a shovel and began to shovel dirt into the well.

Realizing what was happening, the donkey at first cried and wailed horribly. Then a few shovels full later, he quieted down completely.

The farmer peered down into the well and was astounded by what he saw. With every shovel full of dirt that hit his back, the donkey was doing something amazing. He would shake it off and take a step up on the new layer of dirt.

As the farmer's neighbors continued to shovel dirt on top of the animal, he would shake it off and take a step up. Pretty soon, the donkey stepped up over the edge of the well and trotted off, to the shock and astonishment of all the neighbors!

Life is sometimes going to shovel dirt on you, all kinds of dirt. The trick to getting out of the well is to not let it bury you, but to shake it off and take a step up. Each of our troubles is a stepping stone.

We can get out of the deepest wells just by not stopping, never giving up! Shake it off and take a step up!

Have you heard about the fellow who died from drinking a quart of varnish? A horrible end, but a glossy finish!

All those jokes that begin with "these two guys walk into a bar" are pretty silly - wouldn't you think the second guy would have walked around it?

Chuckles

(More) Things that make you go "Hmm?"

- Is it good if a vacuum really sucks?
- Why is the third hand on the watch called the second hand?
- If a word is misspelled in the dictionary, how would we ever know?
- If Webster wrote the first dictionary, where did he find the words?
- Why do we say something is out of whack? What is a whack?
- Why do "slow down" and "slow up" mean the same thing?
- Why do "tug" boats push their barges?
- Why do we sing, "Take me out to the ballgame," when we are already there?
- Why are they called "stands" when they are made for sitting?
- Why is it called "after dark" when it really is "after light"?
- Doesn't, "expecting the unexpected," make the unexpected expected?
- Why are a "wise man" and a "wise guy" opposites?
- Why do "overlook" and "oversee" mean opposite things?
- If work is so terrific, why do they have to pay you to do it?
- If love is blind, why is lingerie so popular?
- Why is bra singular and panties plural?
- Why do you press harder on the buttons of a remote when you know the batteries are dead?
- Why do we put suits in garment bags and garments in a suitcase?
- How come abbreviated is such a long word?
- Why do we wash bath towels? Aren't we clean when we use them?
- Why doesn't glue stick to the inside of the bottle?

Darned if I know, do you ?????

Two oldtimers were sitting on the porch at the farm watching a rooster chase a hen. One of them threw a handful of corn in the rooster's path and the rooster stopped to eat a piece. "Goodness me," said the other oldtimer, "sure hope I never get that old."

Be careful of the words you say.
Do keep them soft and sweet.
You never know from day to day
Which ones you'll have to eat!

A young husband and father returned home from a trip just when a storm hit with crashing thunder and severe lightning. As he wearily came into his bedroom about 2 a.m. he found his two children, sound asleep, in bed with his wife, apparently scared by the loud storm.

Too tired to do anything about it, he resigned himself to sleep in the guest bedroom for the remainder of the night. The next day, he talked to the children and explained that it was O.K. to get in bed with Mommy when the storm was bad, but when he was expected home, he asked that they please don't sleep with Mommy all that night. They said O.K.

After his next trip several weeks later, his wife and the children picked him up in the airport terminal at the appointed time. Since the plane was late, everyone had come into the terminal to wait for the plane's arrival along with the hundred or so arriving passengers.

As he entered the waiting area, his 5 year old son saw him and began shouting: "Hi Daddy! I've got some good news!"

As he waved back, the father said loudly, "What's the good news, son?"

The boy shouted back, "Nobody slept with Mommy while you were away this time."

 *Chuckles*

Thoughts for the day...

If you can't be kind, at least have the decency to be vague.

A penny saved is a government oversight.

The easiest way to find something around the house
is to buy a replacement.

He who hesitates is usually right.

If you can smile when things go wrong,
you have someone in mind to blame.

The sole purpose of a child's middle name is so
he can tell when he's really in trouble.

If ignorance is bliss, why aren't more people happy?

Some mistakes are too much fun to only make once.

I love cooking with wine, sometimes I even
put it in the food.

Everyone has a photographic memory.
Some just don't have the film.

I know God won't give me more than I can handle.
I just wish he didn't trust me so much.

You don't stop laughing because you grow old.
You grow old because you stop laughing.

Dogs have owners....cats have staff.

Camping Tips

When using a public campground, a tuba placed on your picnic table will keep the campsites on either side vacant.

A hot rock placed in your sleeping bag will keep your feet warm. A hot enchilada works almost as well but the cheese sticks between your toes.

The best backpacks are named for national parks or mountain ranges. Steer clear of those named for landfills.

While the Swiss Army Knife has been popular for years, the Swiss Navy Knife has remained largely unheralded. Its single blade functions as a tiny canoe paddle.

Modern rain suits made of fabrics that "breathe" enable campers to stay dry in a downpour. Rain suits that sneeze, cough and belch, however, have been proven to add absolutely nothing to the wilderness experience.

Lint from your navel makes a handy fire starter. Warning - remove lint from navel before applying the match.

You can duplicate the warmth of a down-filled bedroll by climbing into a plastic garbage bag with several geese.

When camping always wear a long sleeved shirt. It gives you something to wipe your nose on.

A potato baked in the coals for one hour makes an excellent side dish. A potato baked in the coals for three hours makes an excellent hockey puck.

The sight of a bald eagle has thrilled campers for generations. The sight of a bald man, however, does absolutely nothing for the eagle.

Bear bells provide an element of safety for hikers in grizzly country. The tricky part is getting them on the bears.

In an emergency, a drawstring from a parka hood can be used to strangle a snoring tent mate.

Our thanks to camper Ann Hughes and her sense of humour for the above tips.

Chuckles

Out of The Mouths of Babes

A first grade teacher collected well-known proverbs. She gave each child in her class the first half of a proverb and asked them to come up with the remainder of the proverb. Their insight will surprise and amuse you!

Better to be safe than . . . . punch a 5th grader.

Strike while the . . . . bug is close.

It's always darkest before . . . . Daylight Savings time.

Never under-estimate the power of . . . . termites.

A miss is as good as . . . . a Mister.

You can't teach an old dog . . . . new math.

*You get out of something what . . . .
you see pictured on the box.*

The pen is mightier than the . . . . pigs.

Where there's smoke, there's. . . . pollution.

A penny saved is . . . . not much.

Two's company, three's . . . . the musketeers.

*Don't put off til tomorrow what . . . .
you put on to go to bed.*

*Laugh and the world laughs with you. Cry and . . . .
you have to blow your nose.*

None are so blind as . . . . Helen Keller.

Children should be seen and not . . .spanked or grounded.

If at first you don't succeed . . . . get new batteries.

Two men were sitting next to each other at a bar. After a while, one guy looks at the other and says, "I can't help but think, from listening to you, that you're from Ireland." The other guy responds proudly, "Yes, that I am."

The first guy says, "So am I!" And where abouts from Ireland might you be?" The other guy answers, "I'm from Dublin, I am." The first guy responds, "Sure and begora, and so am I! And what street do you live on in Dublin?" The other guy says, "A lovely little area it was, I lived on McCleary Street in the old central part of town." The first guy says, "It's a small world, so did I!"

And to what school would you have been going?" The other guy answers, "Well now, I went to St. Mary's of course." The first guy exclaims "The Good Lord must be smiling down upon us! I can hardly believe our good luck at winding up in the same bar on this very night. Can you believe it, I graduated from St. Mary's in 1964 my own self."

About this time, another guy walks into the bar, sits down, and orders a beer. The bartender walks over shaking his head and mutters, "It's going to be a long night tonight, the Murphy twins are drunk again."

Chuckles

A missionary who had spent years showing a tribe of natives how to arm and build things to be self-sufficient gets word that he is to return home. He thinks that the one thing he never did was to teach these natives how to speak English, so he takes the chief and starts walking in the forest.

He points to a tree and tells the chief, "this is a tree". The chief looks at the tree and grunts "tree". The missionary is pleased with this response. They walk a little farther and the Padre points to a rock and says, "this is a rock," at which the chief grunts and says, "rock".

The Padre is really getting enthusiastic about the results when he hears a rustling in the bushes. As he peeks over the top he sees a couple in the midst of heavy romantic activity with much kissing and hugging... The Padre is really flustered and quickly responds, "riding a bike".

The chief looks at the couple briefly, pulls out his blow gun and kills them both.

The Padre goes ballistic and yells at the chief that he has spent years teaching the tribe how to be civilized and kind to each other so how could he kill these people.

The chief replied "my bike".

THOUGHT FOR THE DAY

- Deja Moo! The feeling that you've heard this bull before.

- Clothes make the man. Naked people have little or no influence in society.

- Be nice to your children, they pick your nursing home.

- Happiness is watching a snow plow completely cover a police car.

There was a guy sitting at an airport bar and he noticed a beautiful woman sitting next to him. He thought to himself "Wow! She is so gorgeous, she must be a flight attendant." So he decides to scoot towards her and try to pick her up.

He sits down beside her and says, "Love to fly and it shows??" She gives him a blank, confused stare and he immediately thinks to himself, ooh damn, she must not fly for Delta.

Then he thinks of something else and says "Something special in the air??" She gives him the same confused look. He thinks, damn, she must not fly for American Airlines.

Next he thinks "United" and says "I would really love to fly your friendly skies" whereupon the woman, irritated beyond belief with this guy, barks out "Man, what the hell do you want??"

The man, in a relieved voice, says "Ahhh, Air Canada."

A certain little girl, when asked her name, would reply. "I'm Mr. Sugarbrown's daughter." Her mother told her this was wrong, she must say "I'm Janey Sugarbrown."

The Vicar spoke to her in Sunday School and said, "Aren't you Mr. Sugarbrown's daughter?"

With her mother standing just a few feet away, the little girl replied, "I thought I was, but Mommy says I'm not."

At the beginning of a children's sermon, one girl came up to the altar wearing a beautiful dress. As the children were sitting down around the pastor, he leaned over and said to the girl, "That's a very pretty dress. Is it your Easter dress?"

The girl replied almost directly into the pastor's clip-on mike, "Yes, and Mom says it's a bitch to iron."

Church Signs

(There was a church that had problems with outsiders
parking in its parking lots, so they put up a sign:)

CHURCH CAR PARK - FOR MEMBERS ONLY:
Trespassers will be baptized!

FREE TRIP TO HEAVEN: DETAILS INSIDE!"

TRY OUR SUNDAYS. THEY ARE BETTER THAN BASKIN ROBBINS.

SEARCHING FOR A NEW LOOK? HAVE YOUR FAITH LIFTED HERE !

(An ad for one church has a picture of two hands holding
stone tablets on which the Ten Commandments are inscribed
and a headline that reads:)

"FOR FAST, FAST, FAST RELIEF TAKE TWO TABLETS"

"COME IN AND PRAY TODAY, BEAT THE XMAS RUSH"

"FIGHT TRUTH DECAY, STUDY THE BIBLE"

"HOW WILL YOU SPEND ETERNITY? SMOKING
OR NON-SMOKING?"

One day the first grade teacher was reading the story of Chicken Little to her class. She came to the part of the story where Chicken Little tried to warn the farmer. She read, "...and so Chicken Little went up to the farmer and said, "The sky is falling, the sky is falling!" The teacher then paused and asked the class, "And what do you think that farmer said?"

One little girl raised her hand and said, "I think he said 'Holy Shit! A talking chicken!"

The teacher was unable to teach for the next ten minutes!

Just a Few of The Things I Have Learned From My Children

1. A kingsize waterbed holds enough water to fill a 2000 sq. foot house 4 inches deep.

2. If you spray hair spray on dustbunnies and run over them with roller blades, they can ignite.

3. If you hook a dog leash over a ceiling fan, the motor is not strong enough to rotate a 42 pound boy wearing Batman underwear and a Superman cape. It is strong enough, however, if tied to a paint can, to spread paint on all four walls of a 20 by 20 foot room.

4. You should not throw baseballs up when the ceiling fan is on. A ceiling fan can hit a baseball a long way.

5. The glass in windows (even double pane) doesn't stop a baseball hit by a ceiling fan.

6. When you hear a toilet flush followed by the words "Uh-oh"... it's already too late.

7. Brake fluid mixed with Clorox makes smoke, and lots of it.

8. A six year old can start a fire with a flint rock even though a 36 year old man says they can only do it in the movies.

9. Certain size Legos will pass through the digestive tract of a four year old.

10. Garbage bags do not make good parachutes.

11. No matter how much Jell-O you put in a swimming pool, you still can't walk on water.

12. Pool filters do not like Jell-O.

Chuckles

Sven and Ole worked together and both were laid off, so off they went to the unemployment office. Asked his occupation, Ole said, "Panty stitcher: I sew the elastic onto cotton panties."

Finding it classified as unskilled labour, she gave him $300 a week unemployment pay.

Sven was asked his occupation. "Diesel fitter." he replied. Since diesel fitter was a skilled job, the clerk gave Sven $500 a week. When Ole found out, he was furious!

He stormed back into the unemployment office to find out why his friend and co-worker was collecting twice his pay.

The clerk explained that panty stitchers were unskilled and diesel fitters were skilled labour.

"What skill?" yelled Ole. "I sew the elastic on, Sven pulls it over his head and says....Yep, diesel fitter."

SIGN IN THE BATHROOM OF A RECENTLY RENOVATED BUILDING "ECONOMICAL LOW FLUSH TOILETS - PLEASE FLUSH TWICE".

☺ THOUGHT FOR THE DAY: *It isn't easy to take problems one at a time -- especially when they refuse to get in line.*

A young lady's car had stalled at a traffic light. She tried desperately to start her engine, unsuccessfully. The light turned green while behind her an impatient citizen honked and honked his horn continually. Finally, she got out and walked back. "I'm awfully sorry, but I can't start my car," she told the driver of the other car. "If you'll go there and start it for me, I'll stay here and keep honking your horn."

Two men went bear hunting. While one stayed in the cabin, the other went out looking for a bear. He soon found a huge bear, shot at it, but only wounded it. The enraged bear charged toward him. He dropped his rifle and started running for the cabin as fast as he could. He ran pretty fast, but the bear was faster and gained on him with every step. Just as he reached the open cabin door, he tripped and fell flat. Too close behind to stop, the bear tripped over him and went rolling into the cabin. The man jumped up, slammed the cabin door and yelled to his friend inside. "You skin this one while I go and get another!"

☺ Best advice to a dieter: No thyself!

☺ Having fun is like buying life insurance - the older you get, the more it costs.

WIFE: What would you do if I died? Would you get married again?"

HUSBAND: "Definitely not!"

WIFE: "Why not - don't you like being married?"

HUSBAND: "Of course I do."

WIFE: "Then why wouldn't you remarry?"

HUSBAND: "Okay, I'd get married again."

WIFE: "You would?

(with a hurtful look on her face.)

HUSBAND: (makes audible groan)

WIFE: "Would you sleep with her in our bed?"

HUSBAND: "Where else would we sleep?"

WIFE: "Would you replace my pictures with hers?"

HUSBAND: "That would seem like the proper thing to do."

WIFE: "Would she use my golf clubs?"

HUSBAND: "No, she's left-handed."

WIFE: - - - - silence - - - -

HUSBAND: "Damn!"

A man in a hot air balloon realized he was lost. He reduced altitude and spotted a woman below. He descended a bit more and shouted, "Excuse me, can you help me? I promised a friend I would meet him an hour ago, but I don't know where I am."

The woman below replied "You are in a hot air balloon hovering approximately 30 feet above the ground. You are between 40 and 41 degrees north latitude and between 59 and 60 degrees west longitude.

"You must be an engineer," said the balloonist.

"I am," replied the woman. "How did you know?"

"Well," answered the balloonist, "everything you told me is, I'm sure, technically correct, but I have no idea what to make of your information, and the fact is, I am still lost. Frankly, you've not been much help so far."

The woman below responded, "You must be in management."

"I am," replied the balloonist, "but how did you know?"

"Well" said the woman, "you don't know where you are or where you are going. You have risen to where you are due to a large quantity of hot air. You made a promise, which you have no idea how to keep, and you expect people beneath you to solve your problems. The fact is, you are in exactly the same position you were in before we met, but now, somehow, it's my fault."

Consider This!

- A truly wise man never plays leapfrog with a unicorn.

- The average woman would rather have beauty than brains, because the average man can see better than he can think.

- The computer can do more work than people because it doesn't have to answer the phone.

- The best way to eat a grapefruit is by yourself.

Chuckles

Out of the Mouths of Babes ...

On the first day of school, a first grader handed his teacher a note from his mother. The note read, "The opinions expressed by this child are not necessarily those of his parents."

A woman was trying hard to get the catsup to come out of the jar. During her struggle the phone rang so she asked her four-year old daughter to answer the phone. "It's the minister, Mommy," the child said to her mother. Then she added, "Mommy can't come to the phone to talk to you right now. She's hitting the bottle."

The little girl was watching her parents dress for a party. When she saw her dad donning his tuxedo, she warned, "Daddy, you shouldn't wear that suit." "You know it always gives you a headache next morning."

While walking along the sidewalk in front of his church, our minister heard the intoning of a prayer that nearly made his collar wilt.

Apparently, his five-year-old son and his playmates had found a dead robin. Feeling that proper burial should be performed, they had secured a small box and cotton batting, then dug a hole and made ready for the disposal of the deceased. The minister's son was chosen to say the appropriate prayers and with sonorous dignity intoned his version of what he thought his father always said:

"Glory be unto the Faaaather, and unto the Sonnn...and into the hole he goooes."

Amusing Quotes

"Instead of getting married again, I'm going to find a woman I don't like and just give her a house."

"Why does Sea World have a seafood restaurant? I'm halfway through my fish burger and I realize, Oh my gosh - I could be eating a slow learner."

"Remember in elementary school, you were told that in case of fire you have to line up quietly in a single file line from smallest to tallest? What's the logic in that? What, do tall people burn slower?"

"Bigamy is having one wife/husband too many. Monogamy is the same."

"You can say any foolish thing to a dog, and the dog will give you a look that says, "My God, you're right! I never would've thought of that.!"

"If a woman has to choose between catching a fly ball and saving an infant's life, she will choose to save the infant's life without even considering if there is a man on base."

Dave Barry

**If Noah had been truly wise
He would have swatted
those two flies.**

Chuckles

A magician was working on a cruise ship in the Caribbean. The audience would be different each week, so the magician allowed himself to do the same tricks over and over again.

There was only one problem with this.

The captain's parrot saw the shows every week and began to understand what the magician did in every trick.

Once he understood that, he started shouting in the middle of the show.

"Look, it's not the same hat!"

"Look, he's hiding the flowers under the table!"

"Hey, why are all the cards the Ace of Spades?"

The magician was furious but couldn't do anything, after all, it was the captain's parrot.

One day the ship had an accident and sunk. The magician found himself in a lifeboat, in the middle of the ocean, and of course the parrot was by his side. They stared at each other with hate, but did not utter a word.

This went on for several days.

After a week the parrot finally said: "Okay, I give up, what'd you do with the ship?"

Advice For The Day

**If you have a lot of tension and you get a headache,
do what it says on the aspirin bottle.
"Take two aspirin".... and .... "Keep away from children."**

Darned If I Know! Do You???

A ten year old, under the tutelage of her grandmother, was becoming quite knowledgeable about the Bible, then one day she floored her grandmother by asking, "Which virgin was the mother of Jesus; the Virgin Mary or the King James Virgin?"

**Automotive engineers in Russia tested castor oil as a possible replacement for diesel fuel.
They eventually ruled it out because the cars had to make too many pit stops.**

Chuckles

Two shipwrecked sailors had been adrift on a raft for days. Desperate, one knelt and began to pray: "Oh Lord, I know I haven't lived a good life. I've drunk too much booze. I've lied and cheated. I've done so many things I'm ashamed of, but Lord, if you'll just save me I promise..." "Hold it," interrupted his shipmate, "don't say another word! I just spotted land."

An engineer dies and reports to the pearly gates. By mistake, St. Peter directs him to go below. So the engineer reports to the gates of Hell and checks in. After a few days the engineer becomes very dissatisfied with the level of comfort in Hell and decides to do something about it. He designs many improvements, and pretty soon they have air conditioning, flushing toilets, and escalators. Needless to say, the engineer is a pretty popular guy.

One day St. Peter calls Satan on the telephone and says, "So, how's it going down there in Hell? Satan replies, "Hey, things are going great. We've got air conditioning, flushing toilets, and escalators and there's no telling what this new engineer you sent me is going to come up with next!"

St. Peter replies "WHAT? You've got an engineer? That's a mistake, he should never have gotten down there. Send him up to me at once."

No way," says the devil, "I like having an engineer on the staff and I'm keeping him !"

St. Peter says, "Send him back up here, or I'll sue!"

Satan laughs uproariously and answers, "Yeah, right, and just where are YOU going to get a lawyer?"

Ever wonder...

- Why the sun lightens our hair, but darkens our skin?

- Why women can't put on mascara with their mouth closed?

- Why don't you ever see the headline "Psychic Wins Lottery"?

- Why is lemon juice made with artificial flavour, and dishwashing liquid made with real lemons?

- Why is the man who invests all your money called a broker?

- Why is the time of day with the slowest traffic called rush hour?

- Why isn't there mouse-flavoured cat food?

- When dog food is new and improved tasting, who tests it?

- Why didn't Noah swat those two mosquitoes?

- Why do they sterilize the needle for lethal injections?

- You know that indestructible black box that is used on airplanes? Why don't they make the whole plane out of that stuff?

- Why don't sheep shrink when it rains?

- Why are they called apartments when they are all stuck together?

- If flying is so safe, why do they call the airport "the terminal"?

"Give me a sentence about a public servant," said the teacher .
The small boy wrote
"The fireman came down the ladder pregnant.
The teacher took the lad aside to correct him.
"Don't you know what pregnant means?" she asked.
"Sure" said the little boy confidently.
"It means carrying a child."

Things My Mother Taught Me

- *To appreciate a job well done* -
"If you're going to kill each other, do it outside.
I just finished cleaning."

- *Religion* -
"You'd better pray that will come out of the
carpet."

- *Logic* -
"Because I said so, that's why."

- *Foresight* -
"Make sure you wear clean underwear, in case
you're in an accident."

- *Irony* -
"Keep crying and I'll give you
something to cry about."

- *Contortionism* -
"Will you look at that dirt on the
back of your neck."

- *Stamina* -
"You'll sit there until all that
spinach is gone."

- *Justice* -
"Someday you'll have kids and I
hope they turn out just like you."

- *Behavior modification* -
"Stop acting like your father.."

- *Envy* -
"There are millions of less
fortunate children in the world
who would give the world to have
parents like you do."

- *Anticipation* -
""You're going to get it when we get home."

- *Medical Science* -
"If you don't stop crossing your eyes, they're
going to freeze that way."

- *Humour* -
"When the lawn mower cuts off your toes, don't
come running to me."

Young King Arthur was ambushed and imprisoned by the monarch of the neighbouring kingdom. The monarch could have killed him but was moved by Arthur's youth and ideals. So the monarch offered him freedom as long as he could answer a very difficult question. Arthur would have a year to figure out the answer. If, after a year, he still had no answer, he would be put to death.

The question: What do women really want?
Such a question would perplex even the most knowledgeable man, and, to young Arthur, it seemed an impossible query. But, since it was better than death, he accepted the monarch's proposition to have an answer by year's end.

He returned to his kingdom and began to poll everybody: the princess, the prostitutes, the priests, the wise men and the court jester. He spoke with everyone, but no one could give him a satisfactory answer. Many people advised him to consult the old witch, only she would know the answer. The price would be high; the witch was famous throughout the kingdom for the exorbitant prices she charged. The last day of the year arrived and Arthur had no alternative but to talk to the witch. She agreed to answer his question, but he'd have to accept her price first.

The old witch wanted to marry Gawain, the most noble of the Knights of the Round Table and Arthur's closest friend. Young Arthur was horrified: She was hunchbacked and hideous, had only one tooth, smelled like sewage, made obscene noises, etc. He had never encountered such a repugnant creature. He refused to force his friend to marry her and have to endure such a burden. Gawain, upon learning of the proposal, spoke with Arthur. He told him that nothing was too big a sacrifice compared to Arthur's life and the preservation of the Round Table. Hence, their wedding was proclaimed and the witch answered Arthur's question thus:

What a woman really wants is to be in charge of her own life!
Everyone instantly knew that the witch has uttered a great truth

and that Arthur's life would be spared. And so it was. The neighbouring monarch granted Arthur total freedom.

What a wedding Gawain and the witch had! Arthur was torn between relief and anguish. Gawain was proper as always; gentle and courteous. The old witch put her worst manners on display and generally made everyone very uncomfortable. The honeymoon hour approached. Gawain, steeling himself for a horrific experience, entered the bedroom. But what a sight awaited him. The most beautiful woman he'd ever seen lay before him. The astounded Gawain asked what had happened. The beauty replied that since he had been so kind to her when she'd appeared as a witch, she would henceforth be her horrible, deformed self only half the time, and the other half, she would be her beautiful maiden self. Which would he want her to be during the day and which during the night?

What a cruel question! Gawain pondered his predicament. During the day a beautiful woman to show off to his friends, but at night, in the privacy of his home, an old witch. Or would he prefer having by day a hideous witch, but by night a beautiful woman with whom to enjoy many intimate moments.

Noble Gawain replied that he would let her choose for herself. Upon hearing this, she announced that she would be beautiful all the time, because he had respected her enough to let her be in charge of her own life.

And so you ask ...**what is the moral of this long involved story about a knight's dilemma?** For the answer to your question put this page up to a mirror and all will be revealed to you.

The moral is: If a woman doesn't get her own way, things are going to get ugly - really ugly!

I'm gonna be a bear !

In my next life, I'm gonna be a bear ...
If you're a bear, you get to hibernate.
You do nothing but sleep for six months.
I could deal with that !
Before you hibernate, you're supposed to eat yourself stupid.
I could deal with that !
If you're a bear, you birth your children while you're sleeping
(who are the size of walnuts) and you wake to
partially grown, cute cuddly cubs.
I could deal with that in a big way !
If you're a mama bear, everyone knows you mean business.
You swat anyone who bothers your cubs.
If your cubs get out of line, you swat them too.
I could deal with that !
If you're a bear, your mate EXPECTS you to wake up growling.
He EXPECTS that you will have hairy legs and excess body fat.

Yup, I could sure deal with that !

A man attempted to enter a fancy restaurant and lounge wearing a shirt open at the collar. The doorman told him that he must wear a necktie to be admitted. The man went out to his car, looked around for a necktie, but couldn't find one. He saw a set of jumper-cables in his trunk. In desperation he tied the cables around his neck, managing to fashion a fairly acceptable looking knot, with the ends dangling free.

He returned to the restaurant and the doorman carefully looked him over, and finally said, "Well, OK, I guess you can come in....just don't **start** anything!

An old farmer had owned a large farm for several years. He had a large pond in the back, fixed up nice picnic tables, horseshoe courts, basketball court, etc. The pond was properly shaped and fixed up for swimming when it was built.

One evening the old farmer decided to go down to the pond, as he hadn't been there for a while, and look it over. As he neared the pond, he heard voices shouting and laughing with glee. As he came closer he saw it was a bunch of young women skinny-dipping in his pond.

He made the women aware of his presence and they all went to the deep end of the pond. One of the women shouted to him:

"We're not coming out until you leave."

The old man replied, "I didn't come down here to watch you ladies swim or make you get out of the pool naked. I only came to feed the alligators."

Moral: Old age and treachery will triumph over youth and skill.

A Sunday school teacher asked her class if anyone knew where God is.

One little girl said, "He's in our bathroom;

my mother is always knocking on the door saying,

"God, are you still in there?"

Chuckles

True-isms

Once over the hill, you pick up speed.

I love cooking with wine. Sometimes I even put it in the food.

If it weren't for stress I'd have no energy at all.

Everyone has a photographic memory. Some just don't have film.

 If the shoe fits.....buy it in every colour.

Going to church doesn't make you a Christian anymore than being in a garage makes you a mechanic.

If you look like your passport picture you probably need the trip.

Bills travel through the mail at twice the speed of cheques.

Some women are a total waste of makeup.

A balanced diet is a cookie in each hand.

Middle age is when broadness of the mind and narrowness of the waist change places.

Men are from earth. Women are from earth. Deal with it.

By the time you can make ends meet, they move the ends.

The Best Lawyer Story of the Year.

A Charlotte, NC, lawyer purchased a box of very rare and expensive cigars, then insured them against fire among other things. Within a month, having smoked his entire stockpile of these great cigars and policy, the lawyer filed claim against the insurance company.

In his claim, the lawyer stated the cigars were lost "in a series of small fires". The insurance company refused to pay, citing the obvious reason: That the man had consumed the cigars in the normal fashion. In delivering the ruling the judge agreed with the insurance company that the claim was frivolous. The judge stated nevertheless, that the lawyer held a policy from the company in which it had warranted that the cigars were insurable and also guaranteed that it would insure them against fire, without defining what is considered to be unacceptable fire, and was obligated to pay the claim.

Rather than endure lengthy and costly appear process, the insurance company accepted the ruling and paid $15,000 to the lawyer for his loss of the rare cigars lost in the "fires".

After the lawyer cashed the check, the insurance company had him arrested on 24 counts of ARSON. With his own insurance claim and testimony from the previous case being used against him, the lawyer was convicted of intentionally burning his insured property and was sentenced to 24 months in jail and a $24,000 fine.

This is a true story and was the first place winner in the recent Criminal Lawyers Award Contest.

Advice for the day: If you have a lot of tension and you get a headache, do what it says on the aspirin bottle:
"Take two aspirins" and "Keep away from children".

THOUGHTS TO PONDER

If money doesn't grow on trees then why do banks have branches ?

Can you cry under water?

How important does a person have to be before they are considered assassinated instead of just murdered?

Why do you have to "put your two cents in" ...but it's only a "penny for your thoughts"? Where's that extra penny going to....taxes?

Why does a round pizza come in a square box?

How is it that we put man on the moon before we figured out it would be a good idea to put wheels on luggage?

Why is it people say they "slept like a baby" when babies usually wake up every two hours or so.

If a deaf person has to go to court, is it still called a hearing?

Why are you IN a movie but you are ON TV?

Why do doctors leave the room while you change? They're going to see you naked anyway.

When you sign up for an exercise class, they tell you to wear loose-fitting clothing. If you HAD any loose-fitting clothing you wouldn't have signed up in the first place!

My husband says I never listen to him. At least I think that's what he said.

Brain cells come and brain cells go but fat cells live forever.

Why is it that our children can't read a Bible in school but they can in prison?

158

How to tell the sex of a fly:

A woman walked into the kitchen to find her husband stalking around with a fly swatter.
"What are you doing?" she asked.
"Hunting Flies" he responded.
'Oh, killing any?" she asked.
'Yep, 3 males and 2 females." he replied
Intrigued, she asked "How can you tell?"
He responded, "3 were on a beer can, 2 were on the phone."

As a senior citizen was driving down the freeway his car phone rang. Answering, he heard his wife's voice urgently warning him, "Herman, I just heard on the news that there's a car going the wrong way on Interstate 77. Please be careful."
"Hell", said Herman, "It's not just one car, it's hundreds of 'em."

Investment Tips
Watch for these corporate consolidations!

Hale Business Systems, Mary Kay Cosmetics, Fuller Brush and W.R.Grace Co. will merge and become: Hale, Mary, Fuller, Grace.

Polygram Records, Warner Bros., and Zesta Crackers will join forces and become: Poly Warner Cracker.

3M will merge with Goodyear and issue forth as MMMGood.

Zippo Manufacturing, Audi Motors, Dofasco, and Dakota Mining will merge and become: ZipAudiDoDa.

FedEx will merge with UPS and become FedUp

Grey Poupon Mustard and Docker Pants are expected to become: PouponPants

Knotts Berry Farm and the National Organization of Women will become: Knott Now.

From the Book of
Doggie Philosophy

The reason a dog has so many friends is that he wags his tail instead of his tongue.
Harry Falk

There are no psychiatrists in the world like a puppy licking your face.
Ben Williams

We give dogs time we can spare, space we can spare and love we can spare. And in return, dogs give us their all. It's the best deal man has ever made.
M. Acklam

Dogs love their friends and bite their enemies, quite unlike people, who are incapable of pure love and always have to mix love and hate.
Sigmun Freud

I wonder if other dogs think poodles are members of a weird religious cult.
Jody Falk

Dogs need to sniff the ground; it's how they keep abreast of current events. The ground is a giant dog newspaper, containing all kinds of late-breaking dog news items, which, if they are especially urgent, are often continued in the next yard.
Dave Barry

Anybody who doesn't know what soap tastes like has never washed a dog.
Franklin P. Jones

If your dog is fat you're not getting enough exercise.

Women and cats do as they please, men and dogs should relax and get used to the idea.   *Robert Heinlein*

If you think dogs can't count, try putting three dog biscuits in your pocket and then giving Fido only two of them.   *Phil Pastoret*

You can say any foolish thing to a dog and he will give you a look that says "Wow, you're right! I never would have thought of that!"   *Dave Barry*

The cop got out of his car and the kid who was stopped for speeding rolled down his window. The cop sarcastically said "I've been waiting here all day for someone like you to go by."
The kid replied "Yeah, well I got here as fast as I could."
When the cop finally stopped laughing, he sent the kid on his way without a ticket.

Did you hear what happened to the scientist who mixed poison ivy and a four leaf clover? He ended up with a rash of good luck!

Chuckles

Questions and Answers from Hollywood Squares

Q. Do female frogs croak?
A. If you hold their little heads under water long enough.

Q. If you're going to make a parachute jump, at least how high should you be?
A. Three days of steady drinking should do it.

Q. Can boys join the Campfire Girls?
A. Only after lights out.

Q. If you were pregnant for two years, what would you give birth to?
A. Whatever it is, it wouldn't be afraid of the dark.

Q. While visiting China, your tour guide starts shouting "Poo! Poo! Poo!" What does this mean?
A. A cattle crossing???

Q. When you pat a dog on its head, he will wag his tail. What will a goose do?
A. Make him bark?

A truck driver was driving along on the freeway. A sign comes up that reads, "Low Bridge Ahead". Before he knows it the bridge is right ahead of him and he gets stuck under the bridge. Cars are backed up for miles.

Finally, a police car comes up. The cop gets out of his car and walks around to the truck driver, puts his hands on his hips and says, "Got stuck, huh?"

The truck driver says, "No, I was delivering this bridge and ran out of gas."

What I want for Christmas !!!

Dear Santa:

I am hereby tendering my resignation as an adult.

I have decided I would like to accept the responsibilities of an 8 year old again.

I want to go to McDonald's and think that it's a four star restaurant.

I want to sail sticks across a fresh mud puddle and make ripples with rocks.

I want to think M & M's are better than money because you can eat them.

I want to lie under a big oak tree and run a lemonade stand with my friends on a hot summer day.

I want to return to a time when life was simple. When all you knew were colors, multiplication tables, and nursery rhymes, but that didn't bother you because you didn't know what you didn't know and you didn't care.

All you knew was to be happy because you were blissfully unaware of all the things that should make you worried or upset.

I want to think the world is fair. That everyone is honest and good.

I want to believe that anything is possible.

I want to be oblivious to the complexities of life and be overly excited by the little things again.

I want to live simple again. I don't want my day to consist of computer crashes, paperwork, depressing news, doctor bills, gossip, illness and loss of loved ones.

I want to believe in the power of smiles, hugs, a kind word, truth, justice, peace, dreams, the imagination, mankind, and making angels in the snow.

So....here's my chequebook and my car keys, my credit card bills and my statements. I am officially resigning from adulthood.

And if you want to discuss this further,

you'll have to catch me first, 'cause - Tag! You're it!

Merry Christmas !

 **Chuckles**

Two aerial antennas meet on a roof, fall in love and get married.
The ceremony wasn't much, but the reception was excellent.

Two hydrogen atoms walk into a bar. One says, "I've lost my electron." The other says, "Are you sure?"
The first replies, "Yes, I'm positive."

A man walks into a bar with a slab of asphalt under his arm and says: "A beer please, and one for the road."

Two cows standing next to each other in a field, Daisy says to Dolly, "I was artificially inseminated this morning." "I don't believe you" says Dolly. "It's true, no bull!" exclaimed Daisy.

An invisible man marries an invisible woman.
The kids were nothing to look at either.

A man takes his Rottweiler to the vet and says "My dog's cross-eyed, is there anything you can do for him?"
"Well" says the vet, "let's have a look at him."
So he picks the dog up and examines his eyes, then checks his teeth. Finally, he says, "I'm going to have to put him down."
"What, because he's cross-eyed?"
"No" says the vet, "because he's really heavy."

I went to the butcher's the other day and tried to bet him 50 bucks that he couldn't reach the meat off the top shelf.
He said, "No thanks, the steaks are too high."

I went to a seafood disco last week and pulled a mussel.

Two Eskimos sitting in a kayak were chilly; but when they lit a fire in the craft, it sank, proving that you can't have your kayak and heat it too.

What do you call a fish with no eyes? ....A fsh.

Somebody said..........

- it takes about six weeks to get back to normal after you've had a baby. Somebody doesn't know that once you're a mother, normal is history.

- you learn how to be a mother by instinct....somebody never took a three year old shopping.

- if you're a good parent your child will turn out good...somebody thinks a child comes with directions and a guarantee.

- being a parent is boring.....somebody never rode in a car driven by a teenager with a driver's permit.

- you don't need an education to be a parent...somebody never helped a fourth grader with his homework.

- a mother can find all the answers to her child-rearing questions in books....somebody never had a child stuff beans up his nose or in his ears.

- a mother can stop worrying after her child gets married...somebody doesn't know that marriage adds a new son or daughter-in-law to a mother's heartstrings.

- a mother's job is done when her last child leaves home...somebody never had grandchildren.

- that TV was a wonderful learning tool for children.....

A grandmother was surprised by her 7 year old grandson one morning. He made her coffee. She drank what was the worst coffee of her life. When she got to the bottom, there were three of those little green army men in the cup. She said "Honey, what are these army men doing in my coffee?" Her grandson said "Grandma, it says on TV that the best part of waking up is soldiers in your cup."

Chuckles

A fellow calls 911...

"Hello, is this the RCMP?" "Yes, what do you want?"

"I'm calling to report my neighbour, Mike Fitzpatrick.
He's hiding marijuana inside his firewood.

"Thank you very much for the call sir."

The next day the RCMP officers descended on Mike's house. They searched the shed where the firewood was kept. Using axes, they busted open every piece of wood but found no marijuana.

They swore at Mike and left.

The next day the phone rang at Mike's house.

"Hey Mike - Did the RCMP come to your house?"

"Yeah!"

"Did they chop up your firewood?"

"Yeah!"

"Merry Christmas, buddy!"

NOTICE IN A FARMER'S FIELD

"The farmer allows walkers to cross the field for free but the bull charges."

People want the front of the bus, the back of the church
and the center of attention.

The only time the world beats a path to your door is
when you're in the bathroom.

As we slide down the banister of life
may the splinters never point the wrong way.

An able-bodied seaman met a pirate in a bar and they took turns recounting their adventures at sea.

Noting the pirate's peg-leg, hook and eye patch, the seaman asked "So how did you end up with the peg-leg?"

The pirate replied, "We was caught in a monster storm off the Cape and a giant wave swept me overboard. Just as they were pullin' me out of the water a school of sharks appeared and one of 'em bit me leg off."

"Blimey!" said the seaman.

"What about the hook?"

"Ahhh...," mused the pirate, "we were boardin' a trader ship, pistols blastin' and swords swingin' this way and that. In the fracas, me hand got chopped off!"

"Zounds!" remarked the seaman.

"And how came ye by the eye patch?"

"A seagull droppin' fell into me eye" answered the pirate.

"You lost your eye from a seagull dropping?" the sailor asked incredulously.

"Well...said the pirate...it was the first day with the hook."

Sunday Humour

A pastor got up one Sunday and announced to his congregation: "I have good news and bad news. The good news is, we have enough money to pay for our new building program. The bad news is, it's still out there in your pockets."

While driving in Pennsylvania, a family caught up to an Amish carriage. The owner of the carriage obviously had a sense of humour, because attached to the back of the carriage was a hand printed sign..."Energy efficient vehicle: Runs on oats and grass. Caution: Do not step in exhaust."

A minister waited in line to have his car filled with gas just before a long holiday weekend. The attendant worked quickly, but there were many cars ahead of him in front of the service station. Finally, the attendant motioned him toward a vacant pump. "Reverend" said the young man, "sorry about the delay. It seems as if everyone waits until the last minute to get ready for a long trip." The minister chuckled, "I know what you mean. It's the same in my business.

A minister parked his car in a no-parking zone in a large city because he was short of time and couldn't find a space with a meter. Then he put a note under the windshield wiper that read: "I have circled the block 10 times. If I don't park here I'll miss my appointment. Forgive us our trespasses."
When he returned he found a citation from a police officer along with this note. "I've circled this block for 10 years. If I don't give you a ticket, I'll lose my job. Lead us not into temptation."

Sunday after church a Mom asked her very young daughter what the lesson was about. The daughter answered "Don't be scared, you'll get your quilt."

Needless to say the Mom was perplexed. Later in the day, the pastor stopped by for tea and the Mom asked him what that morning's Sunday school lesson was about.

He said "Be not afraid, thy comforter is coming."

There was a very gracious lady who was mailing an old family Bible to her brother in another part of the country.

"Is there anything breakable in here?" asked the postal clerk.

"Only the Ten Commandments." answered the lady.

How do you catch a unique rabbit? Unique up on it.

How do you catch a tame rabbit?
Tame way, unique up on it.

How do you get holy water? You boil the hell out of it.

What do you get from a pampered cow? Spoiled milk.

What do you get when you cross a snowman with a vampire? Frostbite.

What kind of coffee was served on the Titanic? Sanka.

Why did the Pilgrim's pants fall down?
Because he was wearing his belt buckle on his hat.

When a panel of doctors were asked to vote on adding a new wing to their hospital, the **Allergists** voted to scratch it, and the **Dermatologists** preferred no rash moves.

The **Gastro-enterologists** had a gut feeling about it, but the **Neurologists** thought the administration had a lot of nerve, and the **Obstetricians** stated they were laboring under a mis-conception.

The **Ophthamologists** considered the idea short-sighted; the **Pathologists** yelled "Over my dead body" while the **Pediatricians** said "Grow up!"

The **Psychiatrists** thought it was madness; the **Surgeons** decided to wash their hands of the whole thing and the **Radiologists** could see right through it!

The **Internists** thought it was a bitter pill to swallow, but the **Plastic Surgeon** said "This puts a whole new face on the matter."

The **Podiatrists** thought it was a step forward, but the **Urologists** felt the scheme wouldn't hold water.

The **Anesthesiologists** thought the whole idea was a gas, and the **Cardiologists** didn't have the heart to say no.

A guy comes into a coffee shop and places his order. He says "I want three flat tires and a pair of headlights with a pair of running boards." The waitress, not wanting to appear stupid, goes to the kitchen and asks the cook. "This guy out there just ordered three flat tires and a pair of headlights with a pair of running boards. What does he think this is, an auto parts store?"

"No" the cook says. "Three flat tires means three pancakes and a pair of headlights is two eggs sunny side up and running boards is two slices of crisp bacon."

The waitress thinks about this and then she spoons up a bowl of beans and gives it to the customer.

The guy says, "What are the beans for?"

The waitress replies, "I thought while you were waiting for the flat tires, headlights and running boards, you might want to gas up."

In a small U.S. church the minister was preoccupied with thoughts of how, after the church service, he was going to ask the congregation to come up with more money than they were expecting for repairs to the church building. Therefore he was annoyed to find that the regular organist was sick and a substitute had been brought in at the last minute.

The substitute wanted to know what to play. "Here's a copy of the service" he said impatiently. "But you'll have to think of something to play after I make the announcement about the finances."

During the service the minister paused and said, "Brothers and Sisters, we are in great difficulty; the roof repairs cost twice as much as we expected and we need $4,000 more. Any of you who can pledge $100 more, please stand up."

At that moment, the substitute organist played "The Star Spangled Banner".........and that is how the substitute became the regular organist.

April Fools

This week my phone went dead and I had to contact the telephone repair people. They promised to be out between 8.00 a.m. and 7.00 p.m.

When I asked if they could give me a smaller time window, the pleasant gentleman asked, "Would you like us to call you before we come?"

I replied that I didn't see how he would be able to do that, since our phones weren't working.

Then he requested that we report future outages by email.

I asked him "Does your email work without a telephone line?"

I was signing the receipt for my credit card purchase when the clerk noticed I had never signed my name on the back of the credit card. She informed me that she could not complete the transaction unless the card was signed. When I asked why, she explained that it was necessary to compare the signature I had just signed on the receipt with the signature on the card. So I signed the credit card in front of her. She carefully compared the signature to the one I had just signed on the receipt.

   As luck would have it, they matched!.

In a semi rural area a new neighbour called the local township administrative office to request the removal of the Deer Crossing sign on our road. The reason: "Too many deer were being hit by cars" and he didn't want them to cross there anymore.

I was at the airport checking in at the gate when an airport employee

asked "Has anyone put anything in your baggage without your knowledge?" To which I replied "If it was without my knowledge, how would I know?"
He smiled knowingly and nodded, "That's why we ask."

The convent had been presented with a new car, a red Mini Metro, the pride of its breed. Sister Lucy, the only qualified driver, became the chauffeur. Every Saturday she would drive the Reverend Mother into town for the shopping.

All went well until a holiday weekend when the town was so packed with people and cars that it became evident that there was no earthly place to park.

"Don't worry, Reverend Mother" said Sister Lucy. "You go into the supermarket and I'll drive around the block until you come out."

Off sped the car and the Reverend Mother bustled around the store shopping quickly, then rushing back to the curbside. There she stood for five minutes, ten, twenty...no sign of Sister Lucy. Where could she be?

Eventually the Reverend Mother approached a patrolling policeman. Excuse me, Officer" she said. "Have you seen a nun in a red mini?"

"No," replied the officer, "but these days nothing would surprise me!"

The stoplight on the corner buzzes when it's safe to cross the street. I was crossing with a coworker of mine when he asked if I knew what the buzzer was for.

I explained that it signals blind people when the light is red.

Appalled, he responded "What on earth are blind people doing driving??"

When I arrived at an automobile dealership to pick up our car, we were told that the keys had been locked in it and we found a mechanic working feverishly to unlock the driver's side door. As I watch from the passenger side, I instinctively tried the door handle and discovered that it was unlocked. "Hey" I announced to the technician, "It's open!" To which he replied, "I know - I already got that side."

Tips to Use With Telemarketers

1. If they want to loan you money, tell them you just filed for bankruptcy and you could sure use some money.

2. If they start out with "How are you today?" say, "I'm so glad you asked, because no one these days seems to care, and I have all these problems. My arthritis is acting up, my eyelashes are sore, my dog just died.....

3. If they say they are John Doe from XYZ company, ask them to spell their name. Then ask them to spell the company name. Then ask them where it is located, how long it has been in business, how many people work there, how they got into this line of work, if they are married, how many kids they have, etc. Continue asking them personal questions or questions about their company for as long as necessary.

4. This works great!
Telemarketer: "Hi, my name is Judy and I'm with XYZ Company"
You: Wait for a second; then in a really husky voice ask "What are you wearing?"

5. If the company cleans carpets, respond: "Can you get out blood? Can you get out goat blood? How about human blood?"

6. Tell the Telemarketer you are busy at the moment and ask him/her if he/she will give you his/her home phone number so you can call back. When they say they don't want anyone bothering them at home, you say "Me either!" and hang up.

7. Ask them to repeat everything they say, several times.

8. Tell them it's dinner time and ask them to hold; put them on the speaker-phone and smack your food loudly as you eat. Continue dinner table conversation.

9. Tell them to talk slowly as you want to write everything down.

10. Tell the Telemarketers you are on "home incarceration" and ask if they could bring you some beer.

11. Tell the Telemarketer "Okay, I'll listen to you but I should probably tell you I'm not wearing any clothes."

12. Answer the phone. As soon as you realize it is a Telemarketer, set the receiver down, scream "Oh my God!" and then hang up.

A man decided that he was going to ride a 10 speed bike from Phoenix to Flagstaff, Arizona (about 140 miles). He got as far as Black Canyon City (about 40 miles) before the mountains just became too much and he could go no further.

He stuck his thumb out but after 3 hours hadn't gotten a single person to stop. Finally, a guy in a Corvette pulled over and offered him a ride. Of course, the bike wouldn't fit in the car. The owner of the Corvette found a piece of rope lying by the highway and tied it to his bumper. He tied the other end to the bike and told the man that if he was going too fast, to honk the horn on his bike and that he would slow down.

Everything went fine for the first 30 miles. Suddenly, another Corvette blew past them. Not to be outdone, the Corvette pulling the bike took off after the other. A short distance down the road, the Corvettes, both going well over 120 mph, blew through a speed trap.

The police officer noted the speeds from his radar gun and radioed to the other officer that he had two Corvettes headed his way at over 120 mph.

He then relayed, "...and you're not going to believe this, but there's a guy on a 10 speed bike honking to pass."

A first grade teacher collected well known proverbs. She had twenty-five students in her class and she presented each child in class the first half of a proverb and asked them to come up with the remainder of the proverb. It's hard to believe these were actually done by first graders. Their insight may surprise you. While reading these keep in mind that these are 6 year olds...because the last one is classic!

Don't change horses............until they stop running.

You can lead a horse to water but..........how?

If you lie down with dogs, you'll ....stink in the morning.

An idle mind is...........the best way to relax.

Where there's smoke, there's.........pollution.

Happy the bride who.........gets all the presents.

Don't put off till tomorrow what......you put on to go to bed.

If at first you don't succeed.....get new batteries.

You get out of something only what you....see in the picture on the box.

When the blind are leading the blind ....get out of the way

A miss is as good as ....a Mr.

Love all, trust............me.

The pen is mightier than the.......pigs.

A penny saved is.......not much.

Strike while the...........bug is close.

Don't bite the hand ....that looks dirty.

Two's company, three's.......the Muskateers.

Better late than............pregnant.

TIPS FOR A HAPPY MARRIAGE

Red Skelton shared his humor with us for decades. He did so without four-letter words and raunchy antics. Throughout his career, he gained the respect of his fellow performers and audiences alike, and always was considered a top entertainer in his field. As we deal with our myriad day-to-day problems, a little levity is a welcome respite in today's world. Below are Mr. Skelton's tips for a happy marriage.

1. Two times a week, we go to a nice restaurant, have a little beverage, then comes good food and companionship. She goes on Tuesdays, I go on Fridays.

2. We also sleep in separate beds. Hers is in Ontario and mine is in Tucson.

3. I take my wife everywhere, but she keeps finding her way back.

4. I asked my wife where she wanted to go for our anniversary. "Somewhere I haven't been in a long time!" she said. So I suggested the kitchen.

5. We always hold hands. If I let go, she slaps me.

6. She has an electric blender, electric toaster and an electric bread maker. Then she said, "There are too many gadgets and no place to sit down!" So I bought her an electric chair.

7. My wife told me the car wasn't running well because there was water in the carburetor. I asked where the car was, she told me, "In the lake."

8. She got a mudpack and looked great for two days. Then the mud fell off.

9. She ran after the garbage truck yelling, "Am I too late for the garbage?" The driver said "No, jump in."

10. I married Miss Right. I just didn't know her first name was Always.

11. I haven't spoken to my wife in 18 months. I don't like to interrupt her.

12. The last fight was my fault. My wife asked, "What's on TV?" I said "Dust".

Chuckles

One Sunday morning the pastor noticed little Johnny was staring up at the large plaque that hung in the foyer of the church. The young man of seven had been staring at the plaque for some time, so the pastor walked up and stood beside him and gazing up at the plaque he said quietly, "Good morning, son."

"Good morning, pastor" replied the young man not taking his eyes off the plaque. "Sir, what is this?" Johnny asked.

"Well, son, these are all the people who have died in the service," replied the pastor. Soberly, they stood together staring up at the large plaque.

Little Johnny's voice barely broke the silence when he asked quietly, "Which one, sir, the 8.30 or the 10.30?"

Great T-Shirt Slogans

I used to have a handle on life but it broke!
Beauty is in the eye of the beer holder.
The gene pool could use a little chlorine.
A journey of a thousand miles begins with a cash advance.

Definition of a property dispute: *ground beef.*

A doctor conducting a physical examination noticed bad bruises on the patient's shins.
"Those from playing hockey or soccer?" asked the doctor.
"Neither" replied the patient. "Bridge".

Eight year old Sally brought her report card home from school. Her marks were good...mostly A's and a couple of B's. However, her teacher had written across the bottom:

"Sally is a smart little girl but she has one fault. She talks too much in School. I have an idea I am going to try, which I think may break her of the habit."

Sally's Dad signed her report card, putting a note on the back.

"Please let me know if your idea works on Sally because I would like to try it out on her mother.

Amusing Quotes

A husband is someone who, after taking out the trash, gives the impression that he just cleaned the whole house.

My next house will have no kitchen - just vending machines and a large trash can.

A blonde said "I was worried that my mechanic might try to rip me off. I was relieved when he told me all I needed was turn signal fluid."

When I was young we used to go skinny dipping. Now I just chunky dunk.

Don't argue with an idiot; people watching may not be able to tell the difference.

If raising children was going to be easy, it never would have started with something called labour.

Brain cells come and brain cells go, but fat cells live forever.

THE LITERARY CORNER

"How to Write Large Books" by Warren Peace

"The Lion Attacked" by Claude Yarmoff

"The Art of Archery" by Beau N. Arrow

"Songs for Children" by Barbara Blacksheep

"Irish Heart Surgery" by Angie O'Plasty

"Desert Crossing" by I. Rhoda Camel

"School Truancy" by Marcus Absent

"I Was a Cloakroom Attendant" by Mahatma Coate

"Mystery in the Barnyard" by Hu Flung Dung

"Positive Reinforcement" by Wade Ago

"Shhh!" by Danielle Soloud

"The Philippine Post Office" by Imelda Letter

"Things to Do at a Party" by Bob Frapples

"Stop Arguing" by Xavier Breath

"Raising Mosquitos" by I. Itch

"Mountain Climbing" by Hugo First

Man of the House

The husband had just finished reading the book "Man of the House".

He stormed into the kitchen and walked directly up to his wife, pointing a finger in her face, he said "From now on, I want you to know that I am the man of this house and my word is law!"

I want you to prepare me a gourmet meal tonight and when I'm finished eating my meal, I expect a scrumptious dessert. Then, after dinner, you are going to draw me a bath so I can relax. And when I'm finished with my bath, guess who's going to dress me and comb my hair?"

"The Funeral Director would be my guess" replied his wife.

Rules of Hockey

At one point during a game, the coach called one of his 7 year old hockey players aside and asked "Do you understand what a team is? Do you understand that what matters is not whether we win or lose, but how we play together as a team?"

The little boy nodded yes.

"So," the coach continued, "I'm sure you know when a penalty is called, you shouldn't argue, curse, attack the referee, or call him a pecker-head. Do you understand all that?"

Again the little boy nodded. He continued: "And when I call you off the ice so that another boy gets a chance to play, it's not good sportsmanship to call your coach a dumb idiot, is it?"

Again the little boy nodded.

"Good" said the coach. "Now go over there and explain all that to your mother!"

Don't mess with old ladies!

An older woman gets pulled over for speeding...

Older woman: Is there a problem, officer?

Officer: Ma'am you were speeding

Older woman: Oh, I see.

Officer: Can I see your licence please?

Older woman: I'd give it to you but I don't have one.

Officer: Don't have one?

Older woman: Lost it, 4 years ago for drunk driving.

Officer: I see...Can I see your vehicle registration papers please?

Older woman: I can't do that.

Officer: Why not?

Older woman: I stole this car.

Officer: Stole it?

Older woman: Yes, and I killed and hacked up the owner.

Officer: You what?

Older woman: His body parts are in plastic bags in the trunk if you want to see.

The officer looks at the woman and slowly backs away to his car and calls for backup. Within minutes five police cars circle the car. A senior officer slowly approaches the car, clasping his half drawn gun.

Officer 2: Ma'am, could you step out of your vehicle please?

The woman steps out of her vehicle.

Older woman: Is there a problem sir?

Officer 2: One of my officers told me that you have stolen this car and murdered the owner.

Older woman: Murdered the owner?

Officer 2: Yes, could you please open the trunk of your car?

The woman opens the trunk, revealing nothing but an empty trunk.

Officer 2: Is this your car, Ma'am?

Older woman: Yes, here are the registration papers.

The officer is stunned!

Officer 2: One of my officers claims that you do not have a driver's license.

She digs into her handbag and pulls out the license and hands it to him. He examines the license and looks quite puzzled.

Officer 2: Thank you ma'am, one of my officers told me you didn't have a license, that you stole this car and you murdered and hacked up the owner.

Older woman: Bet the liar told you I was speeding too.

Sitting behind two nuns at a baseball game whose big habits were partially blocking the view...three men decided to badger the nuns in and get them to move.

In a very loud voice, the first guy said, "I think I'm going to move to Utah ...there are only 100 nuns living there."

The second guy spoke up and said, "I want to go to Montana...there are only 50 nuns living there.

The third guy spoke up and said, "I want to go to Idaho...there are only 25 nuns living there."

One of the nuns turned around and looked at the men and calmly said, "Why don't you go to hell...there aren't any nuns there.

Stock market report for today

Helium was up, feathers were down, paper was stationary.

Fluorescent tubing was dimmed in light trading.

Knives were up sharply.

Cows steered into a bull market

Pencils lost a few points.

Hiking equipment was trailing.

Elevators rose, while escalators continued their slow decline.

Weights were up in heavy trading.

Light switches were off.

Mining equipment hit rock bottom.

Diapers remained unchanged.

Shipping lines stayed at an even keel.

The market for raisins dried up.

Coca-Cola fizzled.

Caterpillar stock inched up a bit.

Balloon prices were inflated.

Scott Tissue touched a new bottom.

Sun peaked at midday.

Dawson and his wife, Jennifer, had been debating buying a vehicle for weeks. He wanted a truck. She wanted a fast little sports-like car so she could zip through traffic around town.

He would probably have settled on any beat up old truck, but everything she seemed to like was way out of their price range.

"Look!" she said. "I want something that goes from 0 to 200 in just a few seconds. Nothing else will do. My birthday is coming up, so surprise me!"

Dawson did just that. For her birthday he bought her a brand new bathroom scale.

Nobody has seen or heard from him since.

The Elevator Story

An Amish boy and his father were visiting a mall. They were amazed by almost everything they saw, but especially by two shiny, silver walls that could move apart and then slide back together again by themselves. The boy asked, "What is this, Father?"

The father (never having seen an elevator) responded," Son, I have never seen anything like this in my life. I don't know what it is."

While the boy and his father were watching with amazement, a fat old lady in a wheel chair rolled up to the moving walls and pressed a button. The walls opened and the lady rolled between them into a small room. The walls closed and the boy and his father watched the small circular numbers above the walls light up sequentially. They continued to watch until it reached the last number and then the numbers began to light in the reverse order.

Finally the walls opened up again and a gorgeous, voluptuous 24 year old blonde stepped out. The father, not taking his eyes off the young woman, said quietly to his son," Go get your mother."

A wonderful exercise for mature people

It is suggested doing this exercise three days a week.

Begin by standing on a comfortable surface, where you have plenty of room at each side.

With a 5-lb. potato sack in each hand, extend your arms straight out from your sides and hold them there as long as you can. Try to reach a full minute, then relax.

Each day, you'll find that you can hold this position for just a bit longer. After a couple of weeks, move up to 10-lb. potato sacks. Then 50-lb. potato sacks and then eventually try to get to where you can lift a 100-lb. potato sack in each hand and hold your arms straight for more than a full minute.

After you feel confident at that level, put a potato in each of the sacks.

Politically correct in 2006....

Your bedroom isn't cluttered. It's just "passage restrictive".

Kids don't get grounded anymore.
They merely hit "social speed bumps."

You're not late. You just have a "rescheduled arrival time."

You're not having a bad hair day.
You're suffering from "rebellious follicle syndrome."

No one is tall anymore. He's "vertically enhanced."

You're not shy. You're "conversationally selective."

You're not long-winded. You're just "abundantly verbal."

Food at the restaurant isn't awful. It's "digestively challenged."

Kids don't fail in class anymore. They are just "passing impaired."

Your closet isn't overflowing with junk. It's just "closure prohibitive."

Good Questions???

Q. I've heard that cardiovascular exercise can prolong life, Is this true?

A. Your heart is only good for so many beats, and that's it...don't waste them on exercise. Everything wears out eventually. Speeding up your heart will not make you live longer; that's like saying you can extend the life of your car by driving it faster. Want to live longer? Take a nap.

Q. Should I cut down on meat and eat more fruits and vegetables?

A. You must grasp logistical efficiencies. What does a cow eat? Hay and corn. And what are these? Vegetables. So a steak is nothing more than an efficient mechanism of delivering vegetables to your system. Need grain? Eat chicken. Beef is also a good source of field grass (green leafy vegetable). And a pork chop can give you 100% of your recommended daily allowance of vegetable products.

Q. Should I reduce my alcohol intake?

A. No, not at all. Wine is made from fruit. Brandy is distilled wine, that means they take the water out of the fruity bit so you get even more of the goodness that way. Beer is also made out of grain. Bottoms up!

Q. What are some of the advantages of participating in a regular exercise program?

A. Can't think of a single one, sorry. My philosophy is: No Pain. Good.

Q. Aren't fried foods bad for you?

A. YOU'RE NOT LISTENING!!! Foods are fried these days in vegetable oil. In fact, they're permeated in it. How could getting more vegetables be bad for you?

Q. Will situps help prevent me from getting a little soft around the middle?

A. Definitely not! When you exercise a muscle, it gets bigger. You should only be doing sit-ups if you want a bigger stomach.

Q. Is chocolate bad for me?

A. Are you crazy? HELLO...Cocoa beans...another vegetable!! It's the best feel-good food around!

Q. Is swimming good for your figure?

A. If swimming is good for your figure, explain whales to me.

Well, I hope this has cleared up any misconceptions you may have had about food and diets - and remember,

Life should NOT be a journey to the grave with the intention of arriving safely in an attractive and well preserved body, but rather to skid in sideways - Chardonnay in one hand - chocolate covered strawberries in the other - body thoroughly used up, totally worn out and screaming

WOO HOO! What a ride!